It's another Quality Book from CGP

This book is for anyone studying D&T Product Design at GCSE.

Let's face it, D&T is pretty hard-going — you've got a whole load of technical stuff to learn on top of doing your project.

Happily this CGP book helps to take the headache out of all that learning. We've explained all the technical stuff — and drawn plenty of pictures to make the whole thing that bit clearer. Plus we've stuck in some handy hints to help make your project a winner.

And in true CGP-style it's got some daft bits in to try and make the whole experience at least vaguely entertaining for you.

What CGP is all about

Our sole aim here at CGP is to produce the highest quality books — carefully written, immaculately presented and dangerously close to being funny.

Then we work our socks off to get them out to you — at the cheapest possible prices.

Contents

Section One — The Design Process

Design Brief 1
Research 2
Design Specification 3
Generating Proposals 4
Development 5
Evaluation 6
Manufacturer's Specification 7
Planning Production 8
Design Methods 9
Revision Summary 10

Section Two —Design Skills

What Designers Do 11
Sketching 12
Enhancement — Shading 14
Enhancement — Surfaces and Textures 15
Enhancement — Colour and Mood 16
Perspective 17
Working Drawings 18
CAD — Computer-Aided Design 19
CAM — Computer-Aided Manufacture 20
Recording Stages Using Photography 21
Revision Summary 22

Section Three — Design Influences

Reasons for Designing 23
Design Ideas 24
Product Analysis 25
Social Responsibility 26
The Environment 27
Why People Buy a Product 28
Consumers 29
Design Considerations 30
Labels 31
Health and Safety 32
Choosing the Best Material to Use 34
Revision Summary 35

Contents

Section Four — Materials & Components

Paper and Board 36
Wood 37
Manufactured Boards 38
Metals 39
Plastics 41
Composites and Smart Materials 42
Ceramics 43
Textiles 44
Food 45
Electrical Components 46
Mechanisms 47
Revision Summary 48

Section Five — Tools & Processes

Hand Tools 49
Machine Tools 50
Jigs, Moulds and Templates 51
Deforming 52
Reforming 54
Fabricating — Screws and Bolts 55
Fabricating — Nails, Rivets and Adhesives 56
Fabricating — Joints 57
Fabricating — Joining Metals 58
Fixtures and Fittings 59
Fillers and Finishing 60
Packaging and Waste 61
Revision Summary 62

Section Six — Manufacturing

Scale of Production 63
Manufacturing Systems 64
Control Systems and Feedback 66
Quality Control and Assurance 67
Revision Summary 68

Section Seven — Project Advice

Tips on Getting Started 69
Tips on Development 70
Tips on Evaluation 71
Tips on Presentation 72
Summary Checklist 73

Index 74

Published by Coordination Group Publications Ltd.

Contributors:
Martin Chester
Sharon Keeley
Katherine Reed
Alan Rix

ISBN: 1-84146-795-2

With thanks to Sharon Keeley and Katrina Sharpe for the proofreading.

Groovy website: www.cgpbooks.co.uk

Jolly bits of clipart from CorelDRAW
With thanks to TECHSOFT UK Ltd for permission to use a screenshot from *Techsoft Design Tools — 2D Design* and to PTC for permission to use a screenshot from *Pro/Desktop*

Printed by Elanders Hindson, Newcastle upon Tyne.

Design Brief

The process of designing and making something is called 'the design process' (gosh).
The whole process can take a while — so, like many pineapples, it's usually broken down into smaller chunks.

The Design Process is Similar in Industry and School

It's no accident that the things you'll have to do for your Design and Technology project are pretty similar to what happens in industry.

- The best products are those that satisfy a real need.
- That's why companies spend so much time and money on customer research. The more people there are who would actually use a product, the more chance it stands of being a roaring success.
- The best ideas for Design and Technology projects are also those that meet a genuine need.

The rest of this section describes a typical design process.
It shows the sort of thing that happens in industry every day.
It also shows the stages you need to go through while you're putting a Design and Technology project together.

First get your Idea for a New Product

First things first... whether you're working in the research and development department of a multinational company, or you're putting together your project, you need to explain why a new product is needed.
It could be for one of the following reasons:

1) There are problems with an existing product.
2) The performance of an existing design could be improved.
3) There's a gap in the market that you want to fill.

The Design Brief explains Why your Product is Needed

The design brief explains why there might be a need for a new product.
It should include the following:

1) an outline of the problem and who it affects
2) the need arising from the problem
3) what you intend to do about it (e.g. design and make...)
4) how your product will be used
5) the environment it will be used in

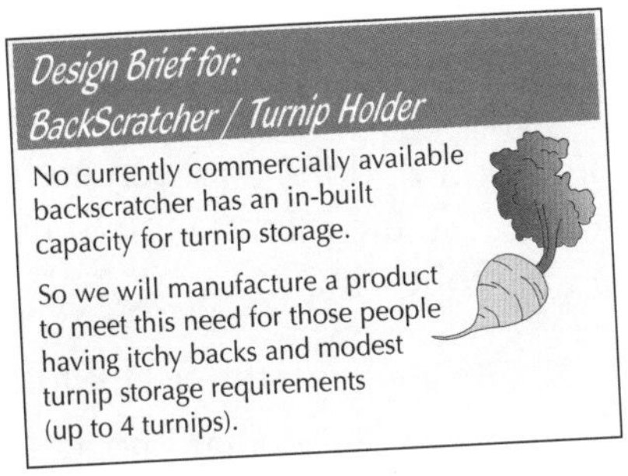
Design Brief for:
BackScratcher / Turnip Holder
No currently commercially available backscratcher has an in-built capacity for turnip storage.
So we will manufacture a product to meet this need for those people having itchy backs and modest turnip storage requirements (up to 4 turnips).

Basically, the design brief should concentrate on the problem you're trying to solve.

Remember — your project doesn't have to involve turnips...

Your design brief should be simple and concise, and allow you room for development. A design brief should not be a detailed description of what you intend to make — you can only say this after you've designed it and tried stuff out. Got that... describe the problem first. The rest comes later.

Research

Once you've written your design brief, you can start researching your project. It's worth doing your research carefully — it can give you loads of ideas for the rest of the design process.

Research Helps you Get Ideas

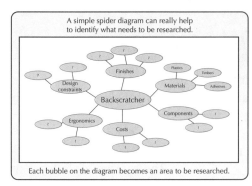

A simple spider diagram can really help to identify what needs to be researched.

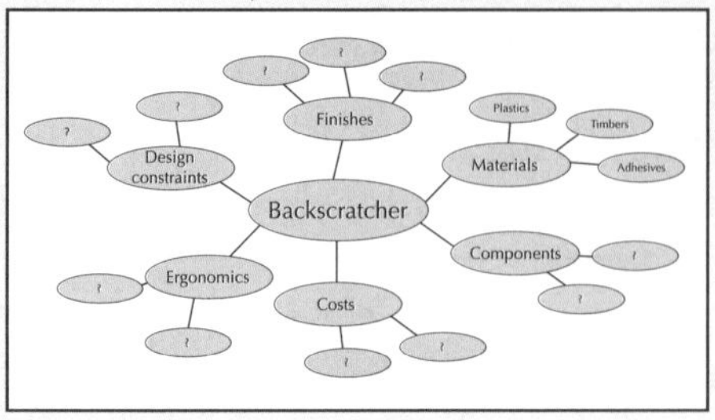

Each bubble on the diagram becomes an area to be researched.

The point of doing research is to:

1) check that people will actually <u>want</u> your product (although you might have done this already when you <u>chose</u> your project).
2) find out what makes an existing product <u>good</u> or <u>bad</u> — talk to people who use this kind of product, and see what they like or dislike.
3) find out what <u>materials</u>, pre-manufactured <u>components</u>, <u>techniques</u> and <u>ingredients</u> you can use, and how they will affect the manufacturing and selling <u>costs</u>.
4) give you a <u>good starting point</u> for coming up with designs.

There are Different Kinds of Research

(1) **Questionnaires** — to find out people's likes/dislikes and so on. This will help you identify your <u>target group</u> and find out <u>market trends</u> (e.g. what things are becoming more <u>popular</u>).

(2) **Disassembling a product** (i.e. taking it apart) — to find out how a current product is <u>made</u> and how it <u>works</u>. It can also give you information about the different <u>materials</u> and <u>processes</u> used, and how <u>existing</u> products meet potential users' needs.

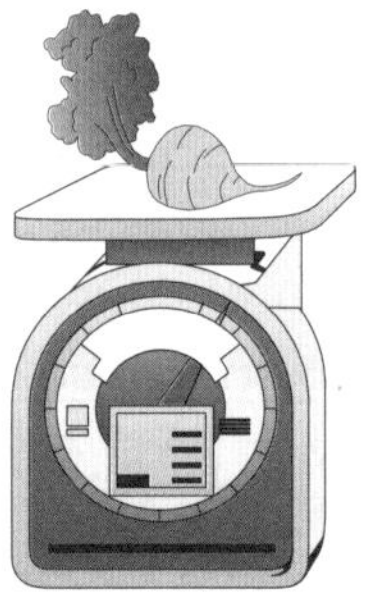

(3) **Measuring** — to find out the <u>weights</u> and <u>sizes</u> of current products. This gives you an idea of the possible size, shape and weight of <u>your</u> product. You could also do some kind of <u>sensory analysis</u> (e.g. you could see how it tastes, feels, looks and smells).

Research Analysis means Drawing Conclusions

Once you've done your research, you'll need to come to some <u>conclusions</u>. This means deciding how to use the information to help you with your design. This is called <u>research analysis</u>.
Do the following:

1) <u>Pick out</u> the useful information.
2) <u>Explain</u> what impact the research will have on your design.
3) <u>Suggest</u> ways forward from the research gathered.

By the time you've done all this, you should have some ideas about how to tackle your project.

I disassembled my dog — he doesn't work any more...

Research is important. Trust me. More important at this stage than cutting wood or moulding plastic. And one more thing while I'm ranting... you could also spend some time doing '<u>book research</u>', e.g. finding out about any British or European standards your product will have to meet.

Design Specification

Now you're ready to put together a design specification. This is a lot more detailed than the design brief and uses all the stuff you learnt during your research.

The Design Specification is a List of Conditions to Meet

1) The design specification gives certain conditions that the product will have to meet. Try to put your specification together in bullet form as specific points, rather than a paragraph of explanations.

E.g. if your research tells you that people would never buy a backscratcher weighing 300 grams or more, then your design specification might include the statement: "Must weigh less than 300 grams."

2) Include points to describe some or all of the following:

- a description of how it should look
- details about what it has to do/be
- materials, ingredients and joining methods
- details of size/weight
- safety points to consider
- financial constraints

Later on Compare Your Designs With the Specification

1) Once you've come up with a design, you need to compare it to the specification and confirm that each point is satisfied.

E.g. If your design specification contains these two points, then all of your designs should be at least 400 mm long and have a variety of colours.

"The minimum length will be 400 mm."
"The product should be multicoloured."

2) Some points might be harder to compare to your specification simply by looking at the product.

E.g. "The product should feel comfortable."

For this, you'll need to get someone to test the product once it's been made/modelled.

You might need to make More than One Specification

You'll probably need to produce several specifications as your project develops:

Initial Design Specification — this is your first design specification. It should be done after your research analysis.

1) As you develop your design, you'll probably want to make some changes to your design specification. This is fine, as long as your design brief is being met and you have taken your research analysis into account.
2) Maybe as a result of some of your modelling (see page 5) you'll find that certain materials aren't suitable. You can add this information to an updated specification.
3) You can keep doing this until you end up with a final product specification.

I'd never buy a backscratcher that didn't glow in the dark...

If I told you that design specifications were going to get your pulse racing, you'd probably suspect I was lying. And of course, I would be lying. To be honest, they're a bit dull. But making a design specification is a vital step in designing and manufacturing a new product. So learn about it.

Generating Proposals

Now hold on to your hats, my wild young things — this is where it all starts to get a bit more interesting. This is the creative bit. This is where you start generating ideas.

There are a few Tricks that can help you Get Started

The following are suggestions to help you get started with designing:

1) Create a mood board — this is a load of different images, words, materials and colours that might trigger ideas for your design stuck down on a big piece of card.
2) Brainstorm — think up key words, questions and initial thoughts relating to your product. (Start off by just writing whatever ideas come into your head — analyse them later.)
3) Work from an existing product — but change some of its features or production methods so that it fits in with your specification.
4) Break the task up into smaller parts — e.g. design the 'look' of the product (aesthetics), then look at the technology involved and so on.

You need to Come up with a Range of Designs

1) You need to annotate (i.e. add notes to) your designs to fully explain your ideas. These notes could be about:

- materials
- size
- user
- shape
- cost
- advantages and disadvantages
- production method
- functions

2) You need to produce a wide range of appropriate solutions that you think could actually be made.
3) Try to use a range of techniques for presenting your designs.

- perspective drawing
- orthographic projection
- cross-sections
- freehand sketching
- digital camera photos
- Computer-Aided Design

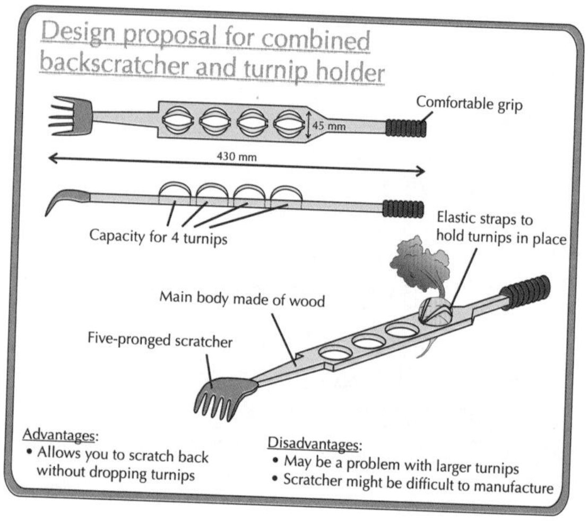

Design proposal for combined backscratcher and turnip holder
Comfortable grip
45 mm
430 mm
Capacity for 4 turnips
Elastic straps to hold turnips in place
Main body made of wood
Five-pronged scratcher
Advantages:
• Allows you to scratch back without dropping turnips
Disadvantages:
• May be a problem with larger turnips
• Scratcher might be difficult to manufacture

4) Once you've got a few possible designs, you need to check that each one matches your specification — any that don't will not be suitable.
5) Finally, you need to choose one of your suitable designs to develop further.

Write whatever comes to mind — no hope for me then...

Think what someone will need to know to fully appreciate your design, and include this information on your proposal. And remember — you need to do quite a few of these so that you can choose the best one to develop and improve. This is the bit where you need to get your creative head on.

Development

Once you've decided on a design, you can begin to develop it further.
This is when your design should start to really take shape.

You can Develop your Design in Different Ways

Depending on the type of product that's being produced, further development might involve:

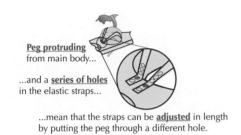

Peg protruding from main body...
...and a series of holes in the elastic straps...
...mean that the straps can be adjusted in length by putting the peg through a different hole.

1) producing further sketches — but in more detail e.g. recording the sizes of fittings and components, and dimensions for component positions. Also sketching how parts should be fitted together.
2) modelling and testing your idea. Or experimenting with different aspects of the design. E.g. you could try various materials, sizes and production methods.
3) using people's opinions about developments to help you arrive at a satisfactory solution.

Modelling means Trying Things Out

It can be useful to make a prototype or model of your idea, especially if it's difficult to draw.

1) Try out different aspects of your design. If your design is quite complex it may help to break it down into smaller, more manageable parts and test them individually.
2) Use a camera (digital or otherwise) to record your models.
3) Evaluate the models (see next page), identifying reasons for selecting or rejecting different designs.

The peg was originally made using a nail, but when the elastic was pulled, the nail came out of the wood too easily.
This was remedied by using a screw.

This is a vital part of the design process. Ideally you should solve all the potential problems with your design at this stage.

Use the Results to Make Modifications

1) Evaluating your model/prototype (see next page) will help you make important modifications (changes) to improve the product, and help it meet the design specification.
2) Suggested improvements could be:
— ways to make the product itself better,
— suggestions to make it more suitable for mass production (see page 63).
3) Once you've made a modification to your design, you'll need to try it out to see if it actually improves things.
4) You might find that you end up trying out lots of different modifications until you find a good solution. That's just the way it goes sometimes.

Modification — wear a parka and ride a scooter...

Modelling and evaluation (see next page) go hand in hand. It's pointless building a model and trying it out if you're not going to bother learning anything from it. So keep your thinking trousers on at all times and make the most of your modelling time.

Evaluation

Evaluation's an important part of the product development process — it means thinking about what's good and what's bad and what you could do better next time.

Keep Records of your Research and Testing

1) As you develop your product, keep records of any testing or market research you do. Write it all down, keep it, and refer back to it.
2) Compare the good and bad points of existing products with your model or prototype. Ask yourself if your product does the job better. Record your results.
3) Find out people's opinions and preferences about your models and prototypes. This will help you to refine your ideas so you can arrive at the best solution.
4) Questionnaires help here — relevant market research questions might include:

- Does the product work well?
- Does the product work as well as similar products on the market?
- Does the product look good? Is it well styled and modern-looking?
- Are you unsure about any of the features? If so, which ones and why?
- If this product were on the market, would you consider buying it?
- If you were buying it, which price range do you think it would fall into?
- Do you prefer another similar product to this one?

This type of evaluation is called formative evaluation — it's being used to help form the final design.

Now You should Know Exactly What You're Making

By the time you've finished developing your ideas and have arrived at a final design, you should have decided:

1) The specific functions and aesthetics of your product.
2) The best materials, tools and other equipment to use (and their availability). This might include identifying any pre-manufactured components you're going to use.
3) The approximate manufacturing time needed to make each item.
4) How much it should cost to manufacture each item.
5) The most appropriate assembly process — this is going to be important information when it comes to planning production, and can be in the form of a flow chart (see page 8).

If you don't know what you're doing now, you never will...

At this stage of the process it should be crystal clear in your own mind how your final product should look, and how you're going to make it. But you're not finished yet. No, no, no, no, no... There's still the little business of actually making your pride and joy. Oh what fun... what fun...

Manufacturer's Specification

Now that you know exactly what you're going to make, you need to communicate all that info to the person who's actually going to make it.

You need to produce a Manufacturer's Specification

A manufacturer's specification can be a written series of statements, or working drawings and sequence diagrams. It has to explain exactly how the product will be made, and should include:

1) clear construction details explaining exactly how each bit's going to be made
2) sizes — precise measurements of each part
3) tolerances — the maximum and minimum sizes each part should be
4) finishing details — any special sequences for finishing
5) quality control instructions — where, when and how the manufacturing process should be checked (see page 8 for time planning and page 67 for quality control)
6) costings — how much each part costs, and details of any other costs involved

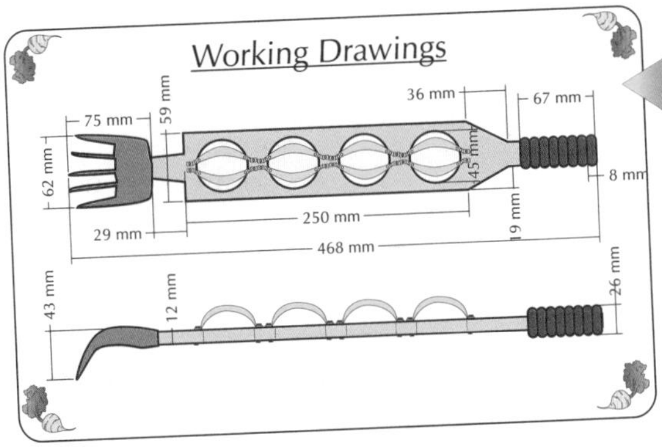

Working drawings give the precise dimensions of the product.

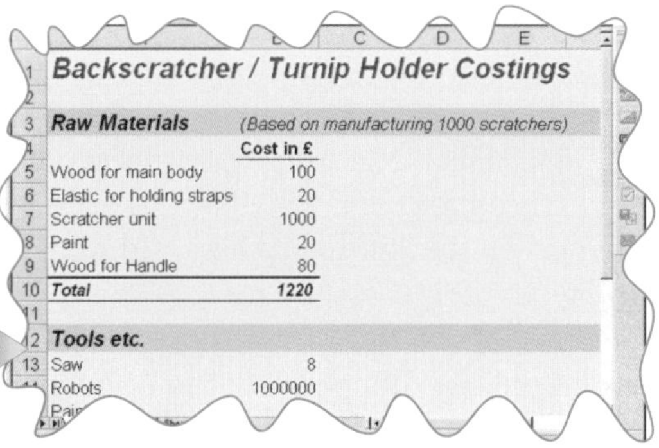

1	**Backscratcher / Turnip Holder Costings**				
2					
3	**Raw Materials**	*(Based on manufacturing 1000 scratchers)*			
4		**Cost in £**			
5	Wood for main body	100			
6	Elastic for holding straps	20			
7	Scratcher unit	1000			
8	Paint	20			
9	Wood for Handle	80			
10	*Total*	*1220*			
11					
12	**Tools etc.**				
13	Saw	8			
	Robots	1000000			
	Pai				

Spreadsheets are great for working out costings.

Plan how long the Production Process should take

When you get to this stage of product development, you also need to plan:

1) how your methods might have to change to produce the product in volume
2) each stage of the process in detail
3) how long each stage will take
4) what needs to be prepared before you can start each stage
5) how you will ensure consistency and quality

See the next page as well for some different ways to help with this planning.

Clear construction details — "Insert tab A into slot B..."*

You know what they say... the devil's in the detail. Yeah, well, I don't know exactly what that means, but it's probably got something to do with being really precise. And that's what you've got to do with your manufacturer's specification, or your masterpiece could end up as a dog's dinner.

*...which doesn't fit, so try it in every other slot before widening slot B until it does actually fit. Repeat for tabs C, D and E.

Planning Production

Making one or two examples of your product is (relatively) easy. But mass-producing it is a whole different ball game. And it takes a shed-load of careful planning.

Use Charts to help you Plan Production

You need to work out how long each stage will take, and how these times will fit into the total time you've allowed for production. There are different ways of doing this:

① **Work Order** This can be produced as a table or flow chart. The purpose of a work order is to plan in sequence each task to be carried out. This will also include: tools and equipment, quality control stages, safety, and so on.

Day	Process	Tools needed
1	Cut main block of wood	Tenon saw
	Cut 4 turnip-holder holes	Drill, fret saw
2	Paint main block of wood	Paint, paint brush

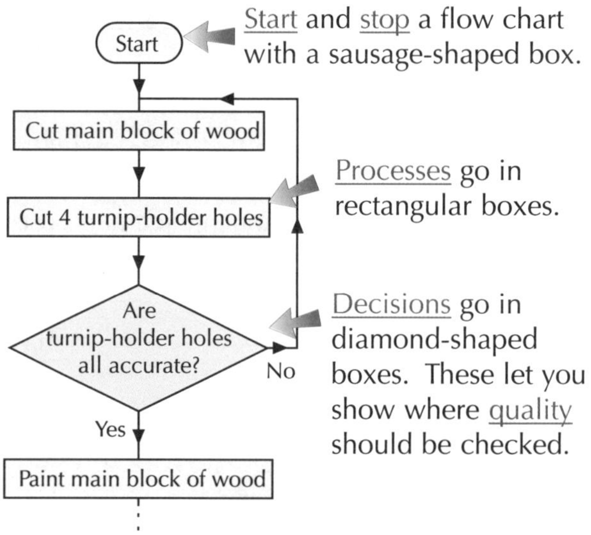

② **Gantt Chart** This is a time plan showing the management of tasks. The tasks are listed down the left-hand side, and the timing plotted across the top. The coloured squares show how long each task takes, and the order they're done in.

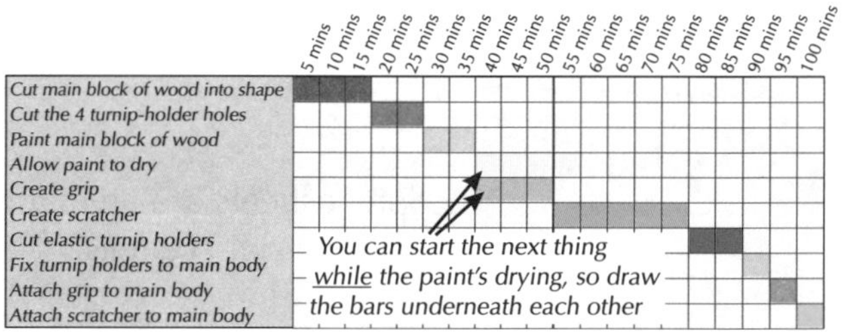

Test that the Product Works and Meets the Specification

1) When you think you've got the final product, it's vital to test it. Most important of all, you have to make sure it works, and meets the original design specification.
2) More questionnaires or surveys may help here. Ask a wide range of people to give their opinions about the finished product.
3) If your product fails to match any part of the specification, you must explain why. You really have to stand back and have a good hard think about your work. If you aren't satisfied with the way any part of the process went, think of how you could put it right for next time.
   Write it down in the form of a report.
4) This type of final evaluation is called summative evaluation — it summarises what you've learnt.

There's nothing like a good chart...

So, in a few short weeks you can do pretty much what it takes people in industry several months to do. You're almost to the end of the section too — one last page on design methods.

Design Methods

There are different ways to approach designing. You can do it by trial and error, or just go with what feels right... or you can do it systematically, step-by-step.

There are Three Different Design Methods

1) **Systematic Design** This means breaking down the design process into a number of different stages and doing each in turn. This is a very orderly and reliable method of designing and the one that you will probably use in school.

2) **Empirical Design** This means using trial and error to develop a good design. For example, making and evaluating prototypes of lots of different designs until you find one which works really well.

3) **Intuitive Design** Designers with a lot of experience can make good guesses about what will work well in a design, and what won't. They use this intuition to help them come up with cool designs.

You don't have to stick to just one of these design methods. Good designers often use bits of all three.

Designing is a Non-Stop Process

The design process doesn't stop when you come up with your first good design. You should be constantly evaluating your design and coming up with improvements.

Identify any problems with the design. Come up with a new design brief. → Develop a new design. → Make a prototype of the design to see if it solves the problem. → Test and evaluate the prototype of your design. → (back to) Identify any problems with the design.

Manufacturers try to Continually Improve Products

1) Manufacturers are always looking for ways to improve the design of their products. This is called 'Continuous Improvement'.
2) Manufacturers want their products to be as good as possible — to make money, to be competitive and to meet standards of product quality such as ISO 9000 (see page 29).
3) Manufacturers might also re-design products in response to customer feedback or advances in technology.

Designs can be improved by making them:

more fashionable	easier to manufacture	easier to maintain	longer-lasting
more user-friendly	safer	more environmentally-friendly	cheaper

"Bye, can't stop — got to keep designing..."

In your coursework use systematic design — because it shows you understand all the different stages of the design process. Know the rules before you break them, as my aunt Bob used to say.

Revision Summary

So that's the section over with, and what a roller-coaster ride full of fun and excitement it was. Yeah, well, the fun's not over yet, so don't look so disappointed. There's still some exciting revision questions for you to tackle. So try the questions, and then have a look back through the section to see if you got them all right. If you did — great. But if you got any wrong, have another careful read of the section and then try the questions again. And keep doing this until you can get all the questions right. That way, you know you're learning stuff.

1) What is the name given to the whole process of designing and making something?
2) Give three reasons why a new product might be needed.
3) Describe the kind of information you should put in your design brief.
4) Give three ways in which research can help you when you're designing a new product.
5) Explain how a questionnaire can be useful when researching.
6) Give two other methods you could use to carry out research.
7) What is the name given to the process of drawing conclusions from your research?
8) Explain what is meant by a design specification.
9) Give five types of information about a product which might be included in a design specification.
10) When would you compile an initial design specification?
11) Give three ways of getting started on your ideas.
12) What does the word 'annotate' mean?
13) What information should you include in your designs?
14) Why should you aim to produce a number of design ideas?
15) Give three techniques for presenting your designs.
16) Name two ways of developing your designs further.
17) Explain why it's useful to model your designs.
18) Describe two kinds of improvement you could make to your design.
19) When should you make an evaluation of your design? a) at the end of the project b) throughout the project c) never — evaluation is for wimps.
20) Describe two ways of evaluating your work.
21) What is meant by the phrase 'formative evaluation'?
22) Explain why a manufacturer's specification needs to be very precise.
23) Give four kinds of information that need to be on a manufacturer's specification.
24) When using a Gantt chart, what information goes down the left-hand side?
25) Describe two methods of planning how long the manufacturing process should take.
26) Describe the process of 'summative evaluation'.
27) Name and describe three different design methods.
28) What is 'Continuous Improvement'?

What Designers Do...

Graphic design is all about communicating ideas through pictures.
This section's all about different ways of doing just that. And it's one rollercoaster ride of fun, too.

You can Communicate Ideas by Drawing

1) Designers communicate their ideas through drawings.
2) The drawings include notes and annotations to explain details.
3) They're used in meetings with clients to explain concepts.

Prototypes are Models of the Product

1) Prototypes are sometimes referred to as mock-ups.
2) They're produced to explain a concept in 3-D.
3) Producing a prototype makes sure the designs are fully understood.
4) They're usually produced to scale.

Find a Gap in the Market to Promote a New Product

1) Before launching a new product, you need to find a gap in the market.
2) This is an area where, at present, there's no product available to meet the customers' needs.
3) The new product then needs to be promoted in a way that looks attractive to the target customer.

Advertising needs to Attract the Customer

1) There are many different techniques used to promote a new product.
2) They include following trends in fashion. This encourages the customer to buy the product in order to appear trendy and up to date.
3) When a friend has bought a product, peer pressure may influence you to buy the product too.

Dan wasn't convinced by the latest fashion trend.

With the CT400, I shall make billions...

You can't just start building as soon as you've had an idea. You need to design it on paper first, thinking about all the details. Then make a prototype to see exactly how it'll look and work. Imagine if I started mass production of my CT400 and then realised I'd forgotten the flush handle...

Sketching

You don't always have to use perfect drawings. Freehand sketches are fine for getting across initial ideas. And they're much easier to do, so you can get new thoughts on paper quickly.

Freehand Sketching is Very Quick

1) Freehand drawing is where you don't use any drawing equipment apart from a pencil or pen.
2) It's the quickest method of illustration and is handy for getting initial ideas down on paper.
3) 3D freehand sketches often show how the whole object would look, while 2D drawings tend to show the details of an object.

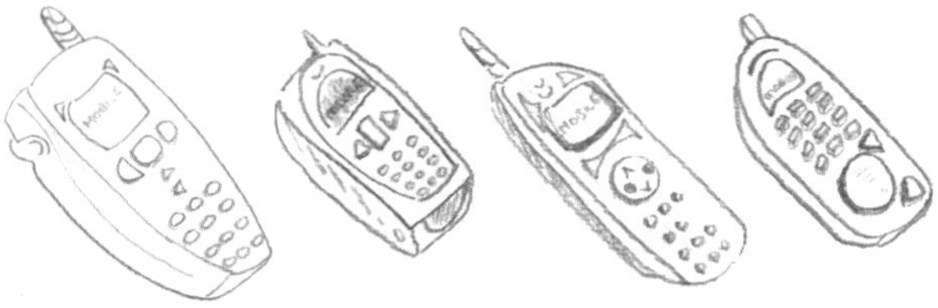

Always Start 2D Sketches with Rectangles and Squares

Standard sketching is very similar to freehand sketching, except that you start by ruling guidelines.

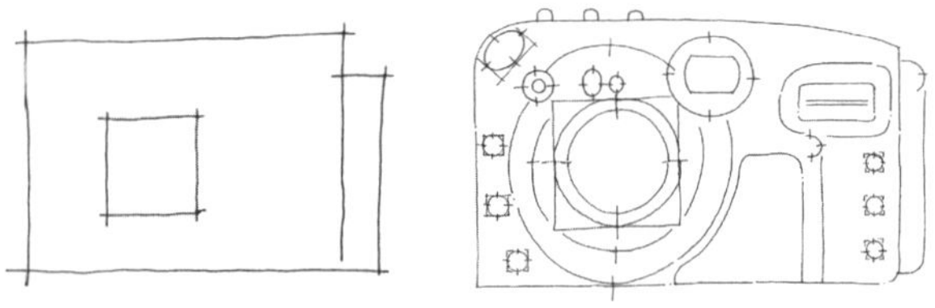

1) Using vertical and horizontal lines you can create squares and rectangles.
2) Use these to draw the outline of your shape first.
3) Details can be added by drawing more squares and rectangles.
4) Add circles and ellipses where necessary.

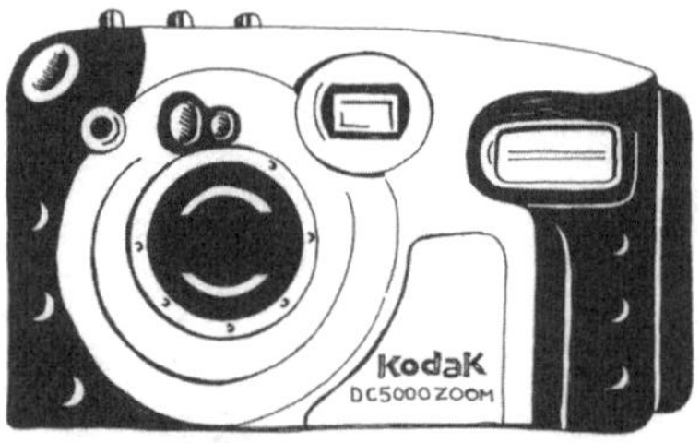

1) Circles are drawn in square boxes and ellipses are drawn in rectangular boxes.
2) Mark half way along each side.
3) Join the points with a curve to form the circle or ellipse.

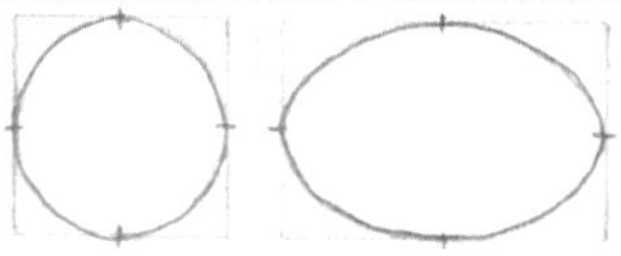

3D Sketches are Done Using Crating

Crating is where you start by drawing a box, or 'crate', then gradually add bits on and take bits off till you get the exact shape.

1) When you're sketching a 3D object, it's easier if you imagine it as a basic shape.
2) First you draw the basic geometric shape faintly.
3) Try to stick to a particular drawing technique like 2-pt perspective or isometric.
4) The object can then be drawn within the box.

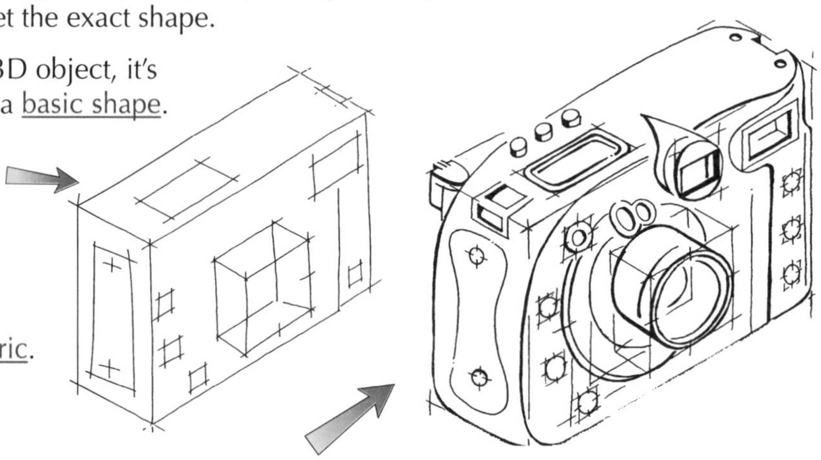

5) Details of the object can be added by drawing more geometric shapes on top.

I love sketching — it's crate...

So remember — always start by drawing the outline of the object. Keep checking the proportions and don't start adding the details until you're sure all the bits are the right size and shape.

Sketching

A designer would use a combination of 2D and 3D sketches. Learn 'em all...

Any 3D Shape can Start Out as a Cuboid

You can remove sections from a cube to make any other 3D shape.

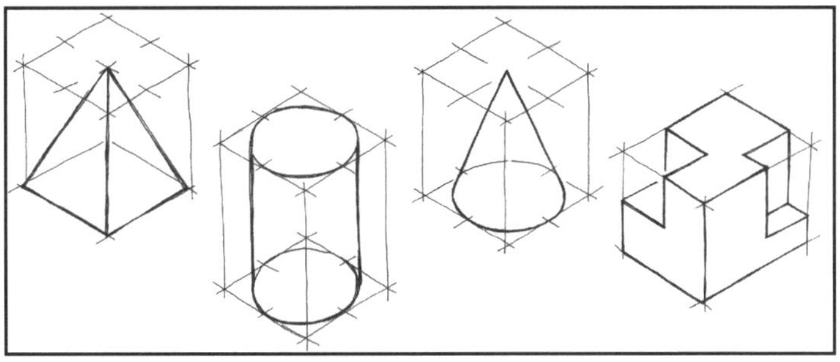

1) Circles and ellipses are completed the same way as in 2D.
2) Draw a square using the chosen drawing technique.
3) Mark halfway along each edge.
4) Join the points.

To Draw More Accurately use a Grid

1) Grids can be laid under your page to improve the accuracy of your drawing. *(Or you could just draw on graph/grid paper.)*
2) You could use an isometric grid, perspective grid or a square grid.

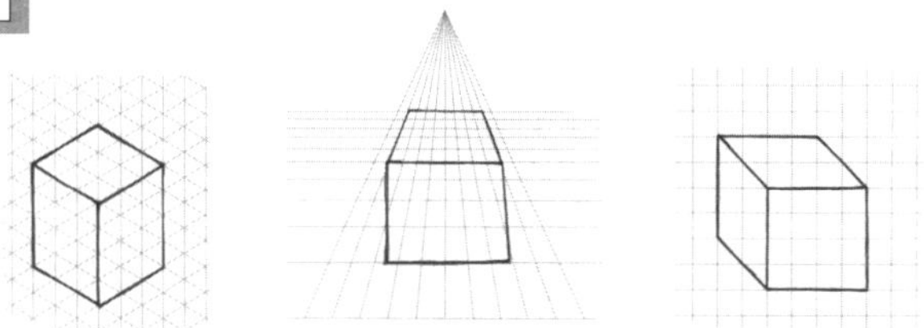

isometric one-point perspective oblique

Wireframe Drawings Aren't Shaded

1) When you draw using the crating technique (see p12), you can leave the solid sides of the shape unshaded.
2) Doing this lets you see straight through the object.
3) You can also view an object in wireframe in CAD software, like the camera shown here:
4) This could be used to show details on all faces of an object.

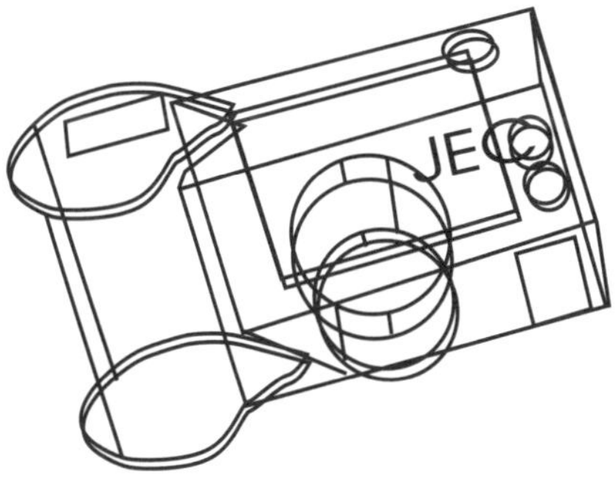

Develop Ideas with Sketches

1) Freehand sketching's very quick.
2) You can combine 2-D and 3-D sketches to explain details.

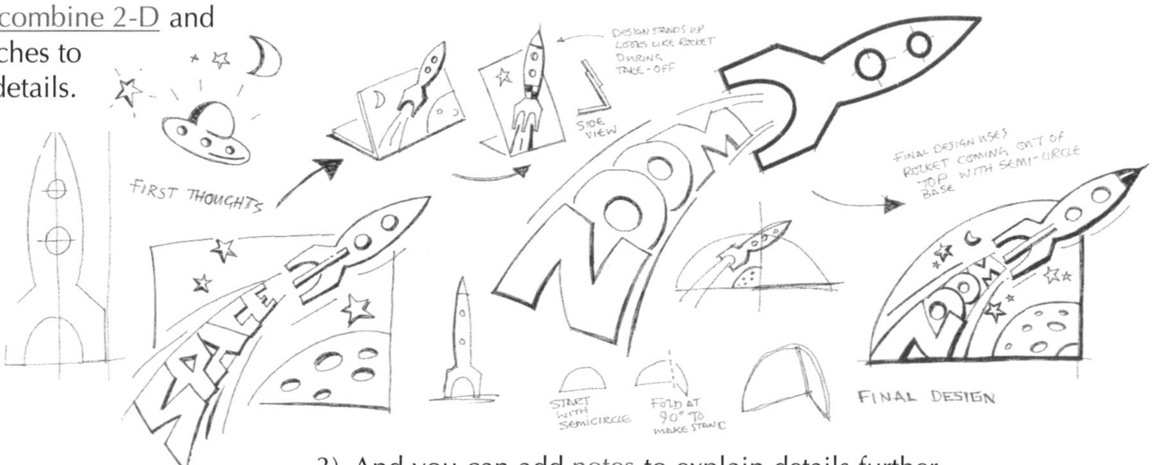

3) And you can add notes to explain details further.

Eeee look at that pyramid — when I last saw 'im 'e were just a cube...

What a funky, groovy and, well, downright sexy page. That's what I think, anyway. Learn the types of sketch here and practise using them — then you can use them in your project. Fantastico.

Enhancement — Shading

You can use various techniques to enhance a drawing.
You can change the thickness of lines or add shading to make parts of the drawing stand out.

Pencil Shading can be Used to Accentuate Shape

1) Shading can be added to a shape to make it look 3-D.
2) Different pencils can be used to create different tones. A soft pencil will create a wider tonal variation.
3) Shading a drawing to show depth, light and shade or texture is called rendering.

4) Think about where the light's coming from — make areas furthest from the light the darkest.

You can Use a Pencil to Shade in Different Ways

1) You can shade shapes using a normal pencil in a number of different ways.
2) Using different types of shading is useful for differentiating parts of an object.

1) When you shade using dots, you need to use a different concentration of dots on each side. Dot-matrix printers use this method, but it's fairly time-consuming by hand.

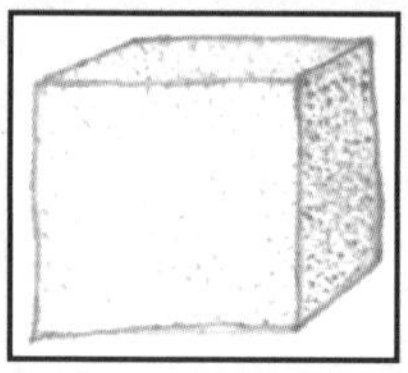

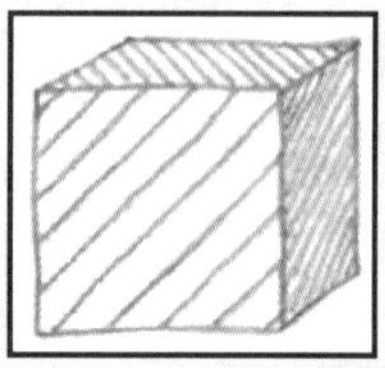

2) In order to shade using lines, you need to use lines at different spacing on each side. Lines at different angles can be used to show different colours, materials, etc.

3) Here's a quick and easy method to give the impression of solidity:
If you can see both surfaces that form a line, draw a thin line.
If you can only see one surface, draw a thick line.

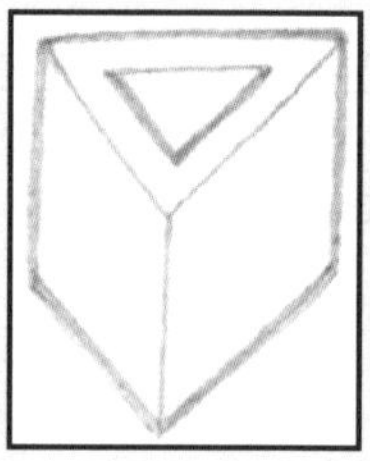

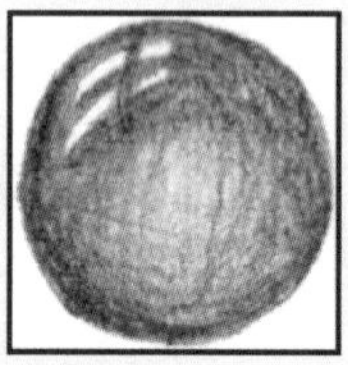

4) Highlights are used to suggest a highly reflective surface. They can be added by leaving white areas.

Could the real Slim Shady please add some highlights to this cube...

This shading stuff's great fun — this *is* Product Design, not maths after all.
But don't forget you still need to learn and practise all this stuff.

Enhancement — Surfaces and Textures

When shading shapes you can also use different techniques to represent different materials — e.g. adding textures, varying the tone and colour, etc.

You can Use Colour and Shading to Represent Surfaces

Wood — use Colour and Draw a Grain...

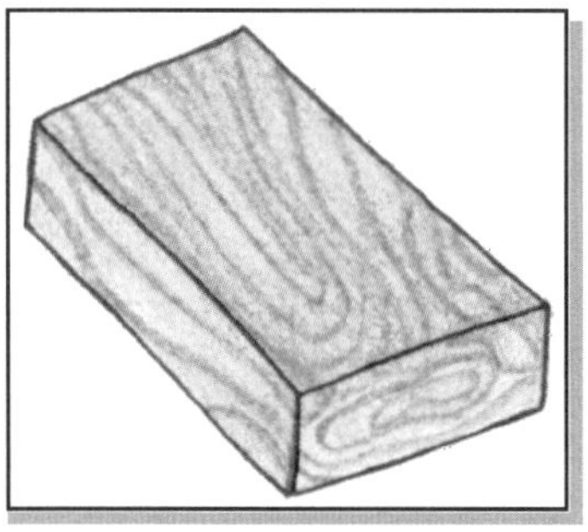

1) Wood can be done using coloured pencils to represent the colour and grain.
2) You can use more than one colour to get the right shade.
3) Wood grain can be added using a darker pencil. Remember that the side grain and the end grain look different.

Metal — if it's Shiny, Draw the Reflections...

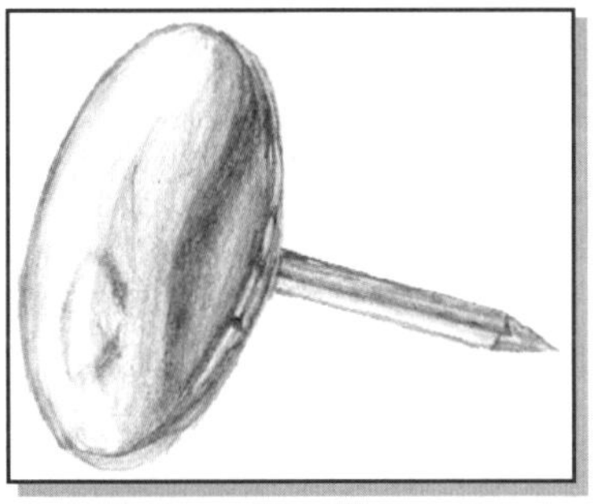

1) Metals can have a variety of colours and finishes.
2) You could have flat sheet metal, or metal with a texture.
3) When shading shiny metal you must be aware of highlights. Try looking closely at a piece of shiny metal in the light. What do the reflections actually look like?
4) Textured metal can be represented using line techniques, e.g. drawing lines to show any ridges, bumps etc.

Plastic — Here's a Few Tricks of the Trade...

1) Marker pens can be used to create the effect of plastic. Alternatively you could use soft coloured pencils or poster paints.
2) Pale coloured marker pens, watercolour paints or pencils or coloured pencils can be used to make an object appear transparent. You may even see objects through the transparent object.

3) Most dark colours look opaque automatically, but you could make a pale coloured material look opaque using watercolour paints by adding a bit of yellow.

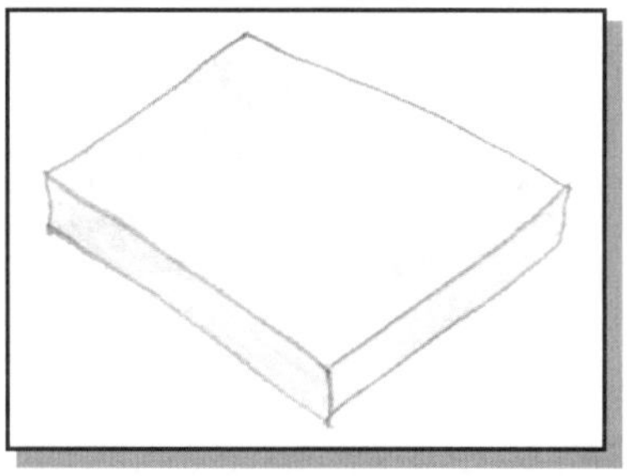

Aaahh — look at the pretty pictures...

Once you've got the hang of highlights, don't restrict yourself to only using them on metals. Anything shiny — glass, smooth plastic or any polished surface — will pick up highlights as well.

Enhancement — Colour and Mood

The use of colour is very important when producing drawings.
As well as being used to make a product aesthetically pleasing, it can be used to represent mood.

Colours can be Organised into Different Groups

1) There are two main types of colour: primary and secondary.
2) The primary colours (red, blue and yellow) can be mixed together to produce any other colour.
3) Secondary colours are colours made by mixing together primary colours.
4) Colour can be represented on a colour wheel which shows you how all the colours fit together.

primary colours: red, yellow and blue
secondary colours: orange, purple and green

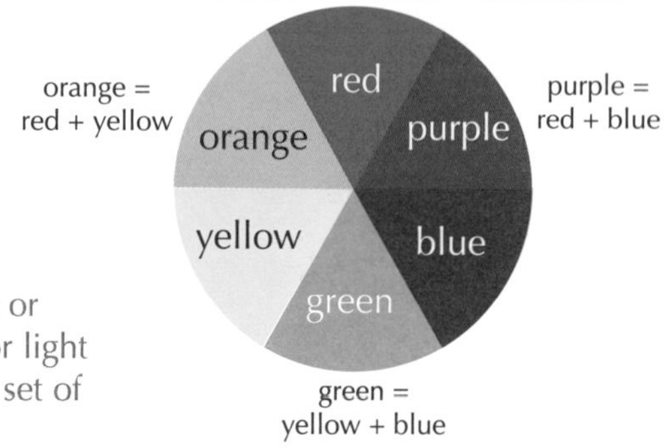

N.B. This colour wheel only applies to paint or pigments — not to light. The primary colours for light are red, green and blue, which gives a different set of secondary colours as well.

Complementary Colours are on Opposite Sides of the Wheel

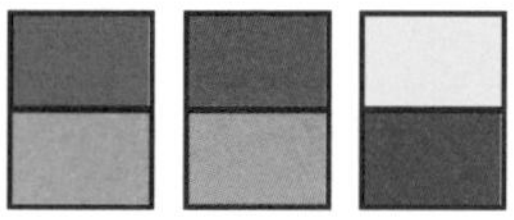

1) Complementary or contrasting colours are found opposite each other on the colour wheel.
2) Examples are red and green, blue and orange, yellow and purple.
3) In CAD packages you can select colours and also edit colours to specific requirements.
4) 'Hue' is another word for 'colour'. It's used a lot in drawing software, e.g. CorelDraw, Photoshop.

Colours can be Used to Represent Mood

1) Different colours can represent different moods or feelings.
2) To create a heavy mood, you might use a dark solid colour while for a lighter mood you'd go for a paler colour.

E.g. the Batman cartoon uses very dark colours to give it a sinister feel, whereas the Peanuts cartoon uses light, pastelly colours which gives a happier, less serious feel to the cartoon.

Mmm...
Nice hot weather...
BRRR...

3) Hot is usually represented by reds or oranges, whereas blues are normally associated with cold.
4) Colours can also represent the mood. For example green is often associated with calm or relaxation, while red often represents anger and conflict.

With all this green I feel so serene.

Top tip 84: Girl/boyfriend too moody? Just hold up the green card...

Works every time. When they're in a real strop and throwing things at you, just hold up the green card and they'll instantly transform into Snow White and start singing sweet melodies about birds, daffodils and goats.

Perspective

"Perspective — well, that's just... um... things being far away, innit..."
Well, kind of, my little pumpkin, but there's more to it than that...

Perspective Drawing — using Vanishing Points

1) Perspective drawing tries to show what something actually looks like — smaller in the distance, larger close to. It does this by using lines that appear to meet at points called vanishing points.
2) These points are in the distance on the horizon line.
3) There are two types of perspective commonly used — one-point and two-point perspective.

One-Point Perspective — for Drawing Objects Head On

1) One-point perspective uses only one vanishing point.
2) The front view of an object is drawn head on.
3) Lines are then drawn to the vanishing point on the horizon line.

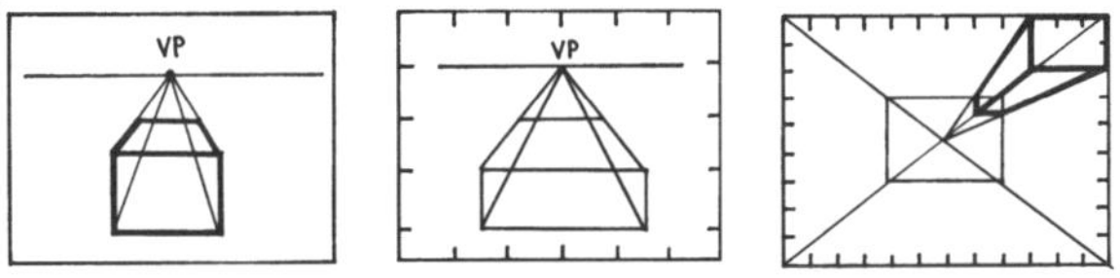

Use a grid to help to draw in proportion.

You've probably seen one-point perspective in cartoons without even realising it...

Two-Point Perspective — for Objects at an Angle

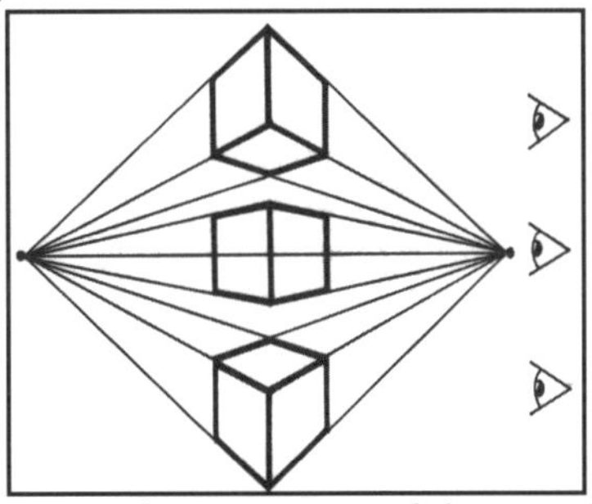

Above the horizon line

On the horizon line

Below the horizon line

The position of the eye level affects how the object appears.

1) Two-point perspective gives a more realistic view of an object drawn at an angle.
2) The horizon line is drawn horizontally across the page.
3) Two vanishing points are marked on the horizon line.
4) The object is drawn by starting with the front edge and then projecting lines to the vanishing points.
5) Remember that vertical lines remain vertical and all horizontal lines go to the vanishing points.

Isometric drawing shows objects at 30°

1) Isometric drawing can be used to show a 3D picture of an object.
2) It doesn't show perspective (things don't get smaller in the distance), but it's easier to get dimensions right than in perspective drawing.
3) There are three main rules when drawing in isometric:

> 1. Vertical lines remain vertical.
> 2. Horizontal lines are drawn at 30°.
> 3. All lines are parallel on regular objects.

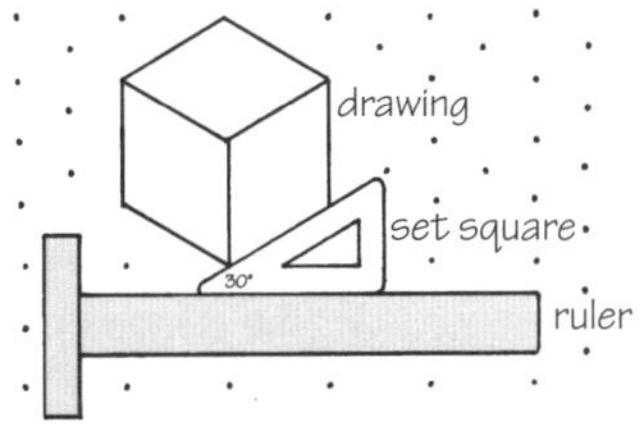

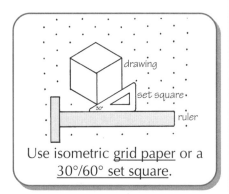

Use isometric grid paper or a 30°/60° set square.

Perspective drawing? — can't see the point in that...

Bit of a stumper — which to use when... OK, quick summary then: perspective drawing is more realistic (2-pt is more lifelike than 1-pt), but isometric drawing is easier (if you use isometric paper).

Working Drawings

Working drawings are for explaining to a production team how to make a product. They include details on sizes, materials and assembly. And they'rrre grrreat...

3rd Angle Orthographic Projection (2D views to you and me)

1) Orthographic projection shows 2D views of a 3D object.
2) All details are shown so the product can be made to the designer's requirements.
3) The front view, plan view and end view of the product are drawn accurately to scale.
4) The symbol for 3rd angle orthographic projection is: 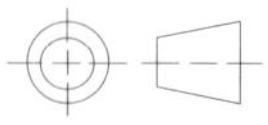
5) To avoid confusion, lines and dimensions must conform to the following British Standards recommendations:

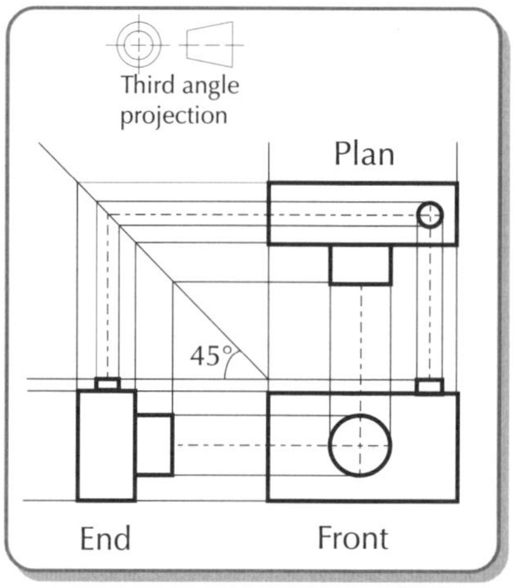

third angle projection of camera

- outlines: thick and continuous
- projection/construction lines: light and continuous
- centre lines: alternate short and long dashes, light
- hidden details: short dashes, light
- dimension lines: medium and continuous

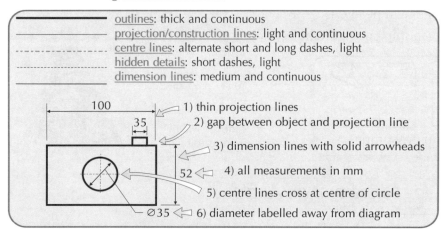

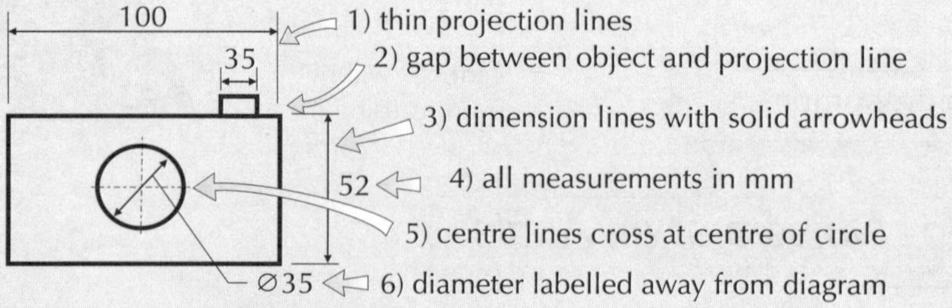

Assembly Drawings show how a Product Fits Together

There are a few ways of showing how things fit together — exploded drawings and sectional drawings are the important ones.

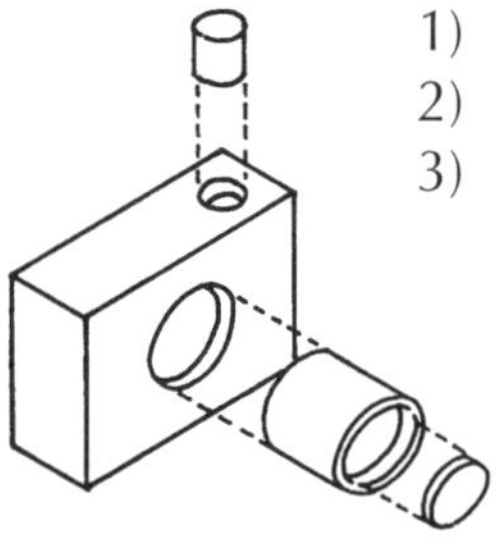

EXPLODED DRAWINGS

1) You draw the product with each separate part of it moved out as if it's been exploded.
2) Each part of the product is drawn in line with the part it is attached to.
3) Dotted lines show where the part has been exploded from.

SECTIONAL DRAWINGS

1) Sectional drawings show additional details.
2) The product is imagined to be cut in half through section X,Y to draw the internal details.

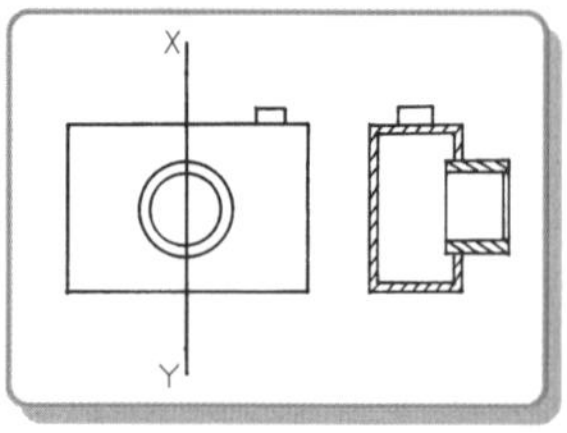

Plan Views Should be Drawn to Scale

1) An area can be drawn to scale to show details of where objects are in relation to each other.
2) They're drawn from above.
3) The scale must be shown clearly as a ratio, e.g. 1:2. With a scale of 1:2 the drawing is half the product's actual size. *(And of course 1:1 is full size.)*

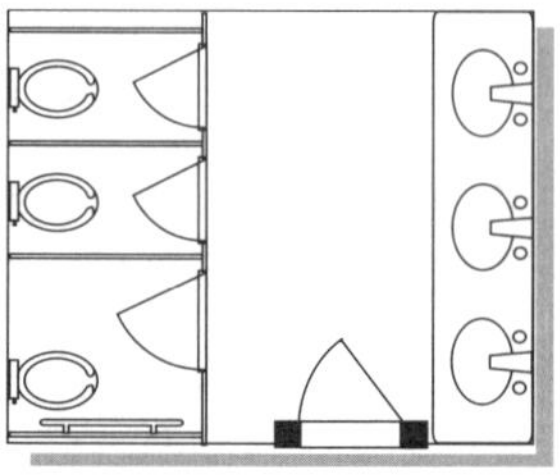
scale 1:100

3rd angle orthographic projection — try saying that 10 times fast...

You need to learn all these details — there's nowt here that you don't need to know. And don't forget to use those British Standards line conventions — might be a pain, but yer stuck with 'em.

CAD — Computer-Aided Design

Almost everything is designed on computer now — washing machines, hoovers, cars, planes, houses, cameras, computers. It's much easier and quicker than doing it all on paper.

CAD — Computer-Aided Design

1) Computer-Aided Design involves designing products on a computer, rather than the traditional methods on paper. Software ranges from 2D engineering drawing programs to 3D frame and solid modelling packages.
2) CAD allows designers to model and compare designs cheaply and relatively easily. Also, many problems can be ironed out before the production of prototypes.
3) In 3D programs, finished products can be viewed from all angles, and scales of components can be worked out in relation to each other.
4) Finished drawings can be printed off on large format inkjet printers or plotters, or can be distributed electronically and instantly to production teams at factories across the world.

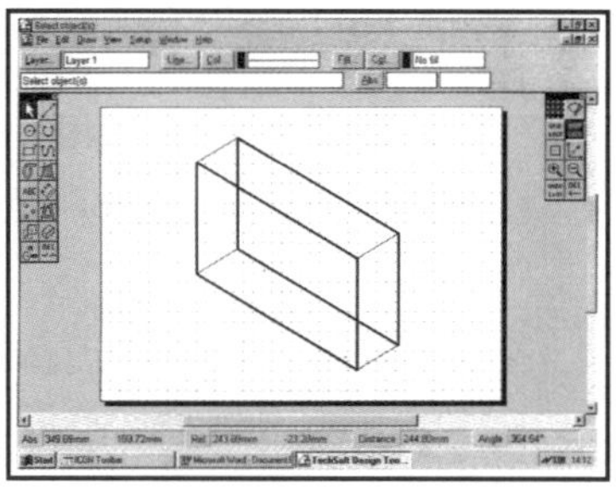

This is 'TECHSOFT DESIGN TOOLS — 2D DESIGN'. (Nice purple background...)

CAD Images can be Changed to Suit the Customers' Needs

1) In order to show specific details, the images can be manipulated in a number of ways.
2) You could show details of dimensions, materials or how the final product will appear.
3) This enables the customer to fully understand the designs and specify any changes before manufacturing.

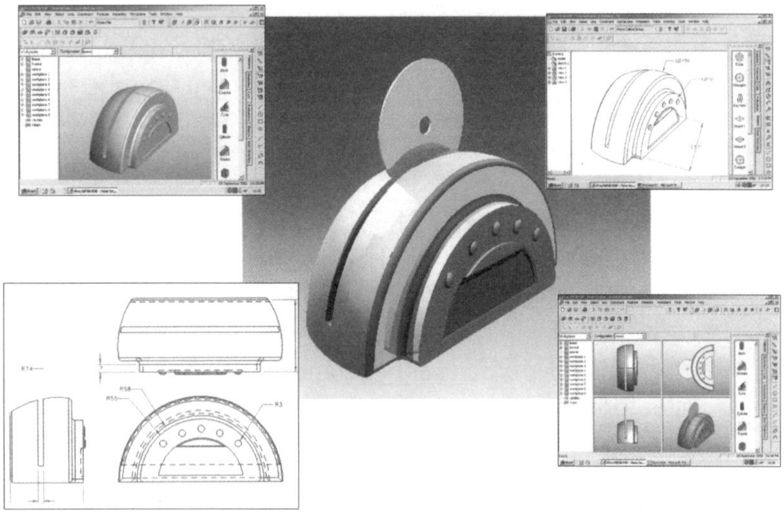

Examples of CAD drawings using Pro/DESKTOP software

CAD has Disadvantages too

1) The initial expense of software and hardware is high.
2) CAD software is often complex — expensive and lengthy training is often needed to learn how to use it.
3) Viruses, corrupt files and power cuts can interrupt and destroy work — just like with all IT-based work.
4) Traditional skills and processes may become obsolete, and jobs may be lost.

Shameless love rat — or IT-facilitated design...

When using a CAD package, save your work regularly in case of power loss or crashing computers. Basic computer common sense, but it's easy to forget once you're well stuck in.

CAM — Computer-Aided Manufacture

CAD is clever, but CAM is really clever. That's what I reckon, anyway.
This is all dead important in industry, and is becoming more important in D&T projects as well.

Computer-Aided Manufacture (CAM) — for Making Stuff

1) Computer-Aided Manufacture is the process of manufacturing goods using information received from a CAD package.
2) Data from CAD software is downloaded into the control unit of a manufacturing machine.
3) Components and products are then made on machines (such as milling machines) which are controlled and operated by computers rather than by a person.
4) Popular makes of CAM machines used in schools include: Boxford, Denford, Unimatics and Roland.

Learn the Advantages of CAM

1) Minor (or major) modifications can easily be made without expensive retooling costs.
2) Repeat jobs can be quickly downloaded and set up — making small batch-produced items cost-effective and feasible.
3) It can save time and labour and reduce errors — again making it more cost-effective.
4) It allows the manufacture of products in situations which may be harmful to humans.
5) Machines can do more complex jobs more accurately and in less time.
6) Machines do not need to rest, so productivity is increased.

But there are some Disadvantages too

They're pretty much the same as the disadvantages of CAD on the previous page.
It all comes down to man versus machine, really.

Machines used in CAM are Computer Numerically Controlled — CNC

1) The machines used in the CAM process are Computer Numerically Controlled.
2) This means the CAD/CAM program works out the necessary movements of the tool head and sends the data to the machine in the form of numbers. The machine's onboard processor interprets the numbers and controls the movement of the tool head.
3) Machines which can be controlled in this way include lathes, milling machines, drilling machines and flame cutters.

the CAMM1 — a CNC cutter and plotter

ADVANTAGES of CNC:

1) Less cost due to less need for separate specialised machine tools for each product.
2) Less chance of human error.
3) The product can easily and quickly be changed without expensive retooling.

DISADVANTAGES of CNC:

1) High initial cost of the machines.
2) High cost of training programmers and operators.
3) Fast special purpose machines are cheaper than CNC machines for large-scale production runs.

My sister's pants were manufactured by a computer — they're CAMiknickers...

Now that people can use CAD/CAM to design things really quickly, it means that they can let their imaginations run wild. There's nothing to lose by trying out lots of different designs on-screen.

Recording Stages using Photography

Photographs are an alternative way of recording information about products or images.
They can be used for research purposes or through the designing stage to record developments.

Take Photographs during your Research

1) You can take photographs to record the original problem.
2) It's worth taking photographs of other things that you'll need to think about during the design process, like the target user.
3) These images can then be stored and used later.
4) If a digital camera is used, the images can be stored on computer and used in presentations and reports.
5) There's also software that lets you play around with digital images to suit individual requirements. For example, colour could be adjusted to show how a product would look with different finishes.

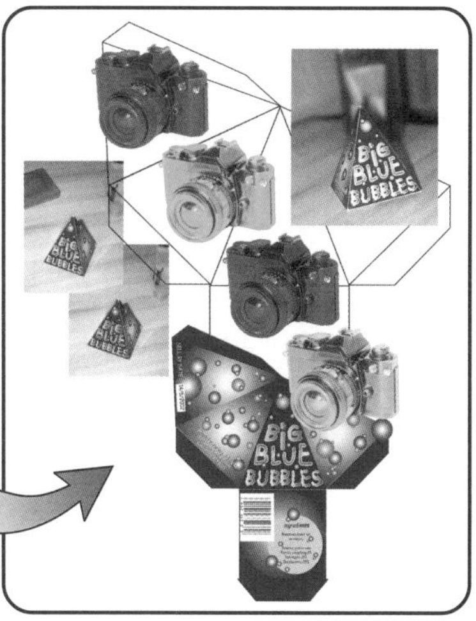

montage of images using Photoshop

Record your Work using Photographs

1) Photographs can be used to record all intermediate stages of the design process, from research through to final outcome and testing.
2) These make a useful record of what's been achieved.
3) The photos can then be used in presentations about the product or to introduce new ideas.

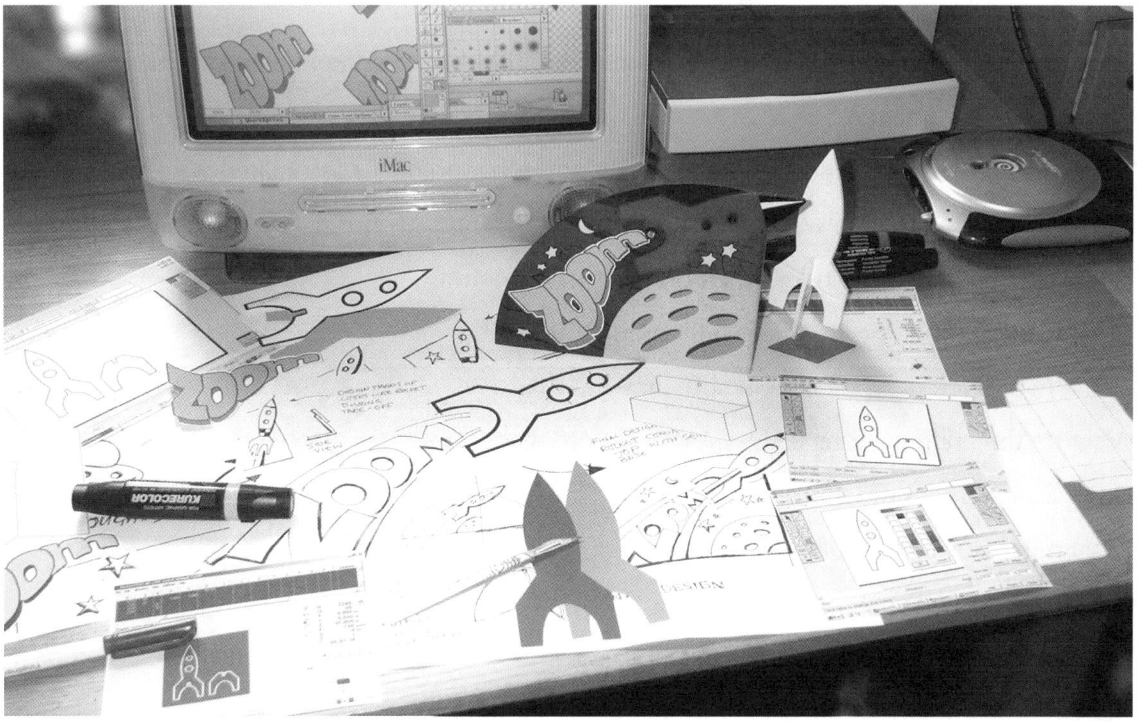

If I had a photograph of you — something to remind me...

...I wouldn't spend my life just wishing... doo doo doodoo doo doo deedoo doo...
Ahem. Sorry, miles away. Yep — digital photos are ace cos you can store them safely on your PC, then if you pour your cup of tea all over your paper copy, you can just print another one.

Revision Summary

Hello again. It's me, the friendly Revision Summary. You may remember me from Section One. You know why I'm here — do all these questions and find out how much you've learned. You can look back at the relevant bit of the section if you get stuck, but keep doing them till you can answer every single question without looking back.
If you can't do these questions, you don't know everything you need to know. Simple as that.

1) What are prototypes and why are they made?
2) Why is it important to find a 'gap in the market' before designing and launching a new product?
3) Suggest one way that you could attract a potential customer to a new product.
4) What are freehand sketches useful for?
5) Explain what 'crating' is.
6) How would you draw a circle or ellipse to the correct proportions when sketching?
7) How and why would you use a grid when sketching?
8) Why might you want to view an object in wireframe?
9) What does the term 'rendering' mean?
10) Give four different shading techniques that you could use to make an object appear 3D. Draw a cube to illustrate each of these methods.
11) Draw three 3D shapes and shade them to look like wood, metal and plastic respectively.
12) Draw two 3D shapes. Shade one to appear transparent and the other opaque.
13) For paints/pigments, what colours are classed as primary colours and which are the secondary colours?
14) What are complementary colours? Give three examples of complementary pairs.
15) What does 'hue' mean?
16) What colour is usually associated with anger and what colour is associated with cold?
17) Explain the difference between one-point perspective and two-point perspective.
18) What are the three main rules when drawing in isometric?
19) What is the symbol for 3rd angle orthographic projection?
20) Name two different types of assembly drawing.
21) What do the abbreviations CAD, CAM and CNC stand for?
22) Give two examples of CAD software.
23) Explain five advantages of using CAD.
24) Give three disadvantages of using CAD.
25) What is CAM? Give three advantages of using CAM, rather than the old-fashioned methods.
26) Explain how photos can be used throughout the design process.

Reasons for Designing

When new products are developed, they are influenced by market pulls and technological pushes. Yep, those poor product designs get as bashed and battered as a haddock in a deep fat fryer.

Market Pull — Making the Products that Consumers Want

1) Market pull is also known as consumer demand. Customers want products that satisfy their wants and needs. Therefore, manufacturers make products that try to satisfy consumers' wants and needs — because if they get it right, they will sell really well.
2) Changing fashions and social attitudes affect what kind of products people want to buy. In other words, consumer demand won't always be for the same things — once manufacturers have satisfied demand for one type of product, consumers will be hankering after something else.

An example of where market pull has influenced the design of a product is with the car. It was invented as a way of transporting people from A to B, but now consumers have made it in to more of a status symbol, demanding luxury extras like air conditioning, and musical entertainment.

In 1959 Sir Alec Issigonis designed the Mini, a popular car design. In 2001 BMW re-launched the New-Mini, and successfully created a new wave of consumer demand — reviving an old design into a modern classic.

Technological Push — Making Products with New Technology

1) Through research and development, new technologies, materials and techniques are constantly being developed. This drives the progression of everyday products.
2) Manufacturers are always looking at ways to improve their products (see page 9). One way they can do this is to use new technology to develop new products, or improve existing ones.
3) Using new technology might make an existing product cheaper, better at its function or better aesthetically — all things which will make products easier to sell.
4) Computers are a good example. They started off as very large mechanical adding machines. Now, thanks to technologies including the micro-chip, they are portable, user-friendly machines.

Telephones are a Good Example

1) Since Alexander Graham Bell first invented the telephone in 1876, its development has been influenced by both technological push and market pull.
2) The telephone is no longer simply a tool for verbal communication, it is now multi-functional. The latest mobile phones use new technology to offer photo and video messaging, e-mail and Internet access, MP3 music and radio.
3) Mobile phones and text messaging have become fashionable — which increases market pull. Mobile phone companies have used marketing to help create consumer demand for more sophisticated and multi-functional mobile phones.

Market Pulling — ask Kat Slater...

Consumers are never happy. If a designer gave them Everest, within a week they'd be going:
"We wouldn't mind a bigger mountain now — maybe in a nicer colour and a bit easier to climb."

Design Ideas

Designers often get inspiration from nature and mathematics. You need to be aware of how these forms, patterns and structures can be used as a starting point for designing and making.

Nature is used as Inspiration for Designing New Products

Nature can be a design inspiration, in terms of the aesthetics, function and structure of a product.

Inspiration for Structure

The massive domes at the Eden Project form a very strong, lightweight structure, just like a honeycomb.

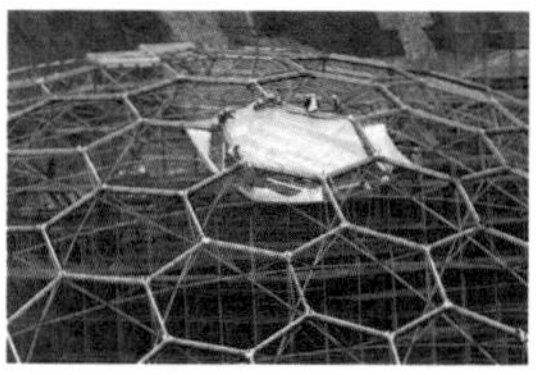

The Eden Project

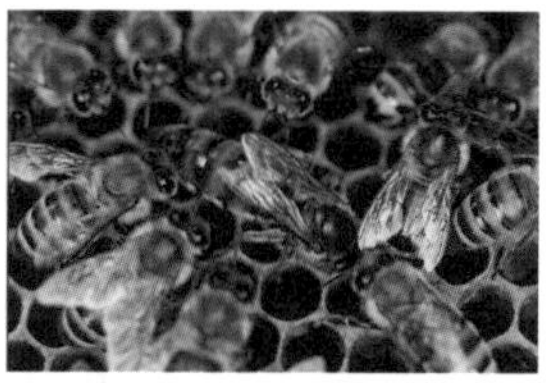

A honeycomb

Inspiration for Function

Cats' eyes were invented in Yorkshire in the 1930s by Percy Shaw, and are now used on roads all over the country. They were inspired by the way cats' eyes reflect in the dark.

Inspiration for Aesthetics

Patterns on textile products often use nature as inspiration, e.g. designs showing flowers, plants and animals.

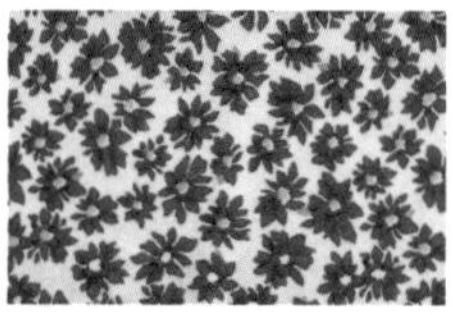

Mathematics can also Provide Design Inspiration

1) Patterns using grids and repeating shapes are often used within product design.
2) Many products, especially packaging, are based on simple geometric shapes such as the square, rectangle, circle and triangle.

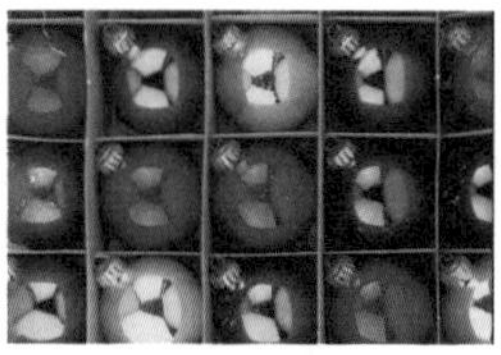

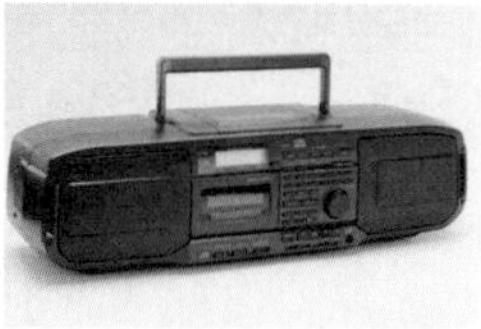

The Fibonacci Series

Fibonacci was a great mathematician born in Italy in about 1170 AD.
He came up with a sequence of numbers called the Fibonacci series.
You start with 0, 1, 1 and keep adding together the last two numbers to make the next number:

0, 1, 1, 2, 3, 5, 8, 13, 21, 34, 55, 89...

If you draw a rectangle using any two adjacent numbers from the series it will look well proportioned.

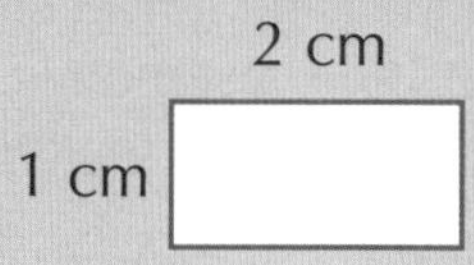

Design — birds do it, bees do it, even Maths teachers do it...

Look at how lovely that little 1 cm x 2 cm rectangle is. What a nice thing to be famous for. Yet, also, how ridiculous. I bet Fibonacci wished he'd done summat more sensible — discovered the potato or starred in 'Easy Rider' or been Madonna or... built a castle out of orange peel using only his toes.

Product Analysis

You've no hope of designing good products if you don't look at other people's stuff first — all designers do it. You need to work out what makes them work and what makes the designs good.

Analysing Existing Products Makes You a Better Designer

Product analysis is essential (for all designers) because it helps you:

1) practise thinking about design — and practice means improvement,
2) get familiar with the manufacturing methods used for different products,
3) understand the uses of different materials,
4) get ideas to use in your own designs, or modify existing designs based on what you find out,
5) pick out examples of good or bad design, manufacture and material selection,
6) make better judgements about what products people might buy.

Consider all the Factors when Analysing a Product

1. FUNCTION: Function is what the product is used for — and how it works. Disassembling (taking apart) a product is very useful for finding out how it works. Take careful notes and record what parts it has and how it's structured, using sketches or photos.

2. FORM: This is the shape and look of the product — e.g. colour, texture and decoration. A product could be old-fashioned or modern-looking. It could have flowing curves or it might be very angled with lots of corners. This is also known as 'aesthetics'.

3. ERGONOMICS: Ergonomics is about how easy the product is to use — whether it's safe and comfortable. For example, a hand-held product needs to fit well in the hand, and controls and buttons need to be easily reachable.

4. COST: You need to consider value for money — whether a product is cheaper or more expensive than similar products on the market.

5. COMPETITION: How a product performs compared to other similar products on the market.

6. ENVIRONMENT: Find out if the design and manufacture of a product is environmentally-friendly, e.g. does it use recycled or biodegradable materials? How are the waste products of manufacturing disposed of?

7. MATERIALS: Product analysis should include looking at what materials have been used, why those materials were chosen and how those materials were formed or shaped.

8. MANUFACTURE: Consider all the processes that have been used to manufacture the product, e.g. which technique was used to mould plastic parts of the product. Check if any parts have been assembled separately and plonked into the product later (called sub-assembly).

9. DEVELOPMENT: Development is stuff that the manufacturer could do to improve the product. Development includes things they could do to make it more popular and increase sales.

Become a better designer — learn when to add go-faster stripes...

Nine factors to learn. That's all.

Social Responsibility

Social responsibility in design is all about making sure you don't make products that mess up people's health, people's lives or the environment. Hmm. Serious stuff.

Design Must Be Socially and Environmentally Responsible

When you're selecting materials, components, and manufacturing processes, think about:

1) Will using the product harm people or the environment?
2) Are any materials used, including paints and varnishes, toxic?
3) Will the manufacture of the product harm the environment? E.g. consider how much waste material will be produced by the manufacturing process, and how it's going to be disposed of.
4) Can recycled materials be used to make the product or packaging? Or biodegradable or recyclable materials if the product's designed to be thrown away after use.
5) Will conditions for workers during manufacture be of a good standard? E.g. making sure manufacturing processes aren't hazardous.
6) Will any social, cultural or religious groups possibly be offended by the product?

How do you flush this thing...

Products Must be Safe and Easy to Use

When you finalise a design, think about how people are going to use the product.

1) The product must be safe to use.
2) The product must be user-friendly. If the product is frustrating and difficult to use, it isn't well designed.
3) Think whether the product could be misused. If people use a product for something that it hasn't been designed for, it might be dangerous.

Ergonomics means Making the Product Fit the User

1) Products need to be designed so that their size and proportions make them fit the needs of the user — e.g. a chair for a five-year-old needs to be a different size from a chair for a fifteen-year-old (obviously).
2) Designers use body measurement data, known as anthropometrics, to make sure that the product is the right size and shape for people to use.
3) For example, a chair seat needs to be the right height off the ground so that the person sitting in it has their feet on the floor, and their knees at a right angle. The back of the chair should support the person's back in the right place.
4) Badly designed products can have long-term health impacts. They might well be safe to use on a day-to-day basis (e.g. there's no risk of losing a limb), but end up causing things like eye strain or backache after long-term use.

There are Social Issues with Products Aimed at Kids

1) Parents have strong views on what sort of products they want their kids to use.
2) Society has an axe to grind, too — e.g. a hand-held games console might be criticised because it encourages kids to sit around all day, hunched over a tiny screen instead of running about and getting fresh air.

Anyone nodded off yet?...

Social responsibility is a bit gloomy, but it's just about making sure that products are the right shape and size for people to use without pain or injury, and that no one is damaged by making them.

The Environment

Humans exploit and use up the Earth's non-renewable resources simply by using so much stuff. We pollute the water and air and produce large quantities of waste. Not very clever really.

The Materials and Processes You Use Affect the Environment

1) The rainforests are a prime example of a threatened resource. They produce valuable and exotic hardwoods which are (mostly) not being replaced. Softwoods (which can regenerate themselves in a person's lifetime) are a greener choice, as are recycled materials that use waste wood,e.g. chipboard.
2) Metal ores are taken from the Earth's crust. There's only a limited amount of each ore.
3) Most plastics come from oil, which will eventually run out.
4) Recycling and using recycled products is environmentally responsible.
5) Energy efficiency is not only green, but cost-effective, too. Manufacturing processes should be chosen for energy efficiency. Renewable energy sources, like wind power or hydroelectricity, are the best for the Environment. Manufacturers can choose to site factories where renewable energy is available.

Throwing Away Old Products Causes Pollution

1) At the end of its life, an old product needs to be disposed of to make way for a shiny new one. Most waste goes into landfill sites. Some chemicals used in products cause serious problems when they get into watercourses or into the soil. There are laws about what can be dumped into landfill sites — and what has to be recycled or specially treated to make it safe.
2) Britain's recycling rate stands at 11% — which is about a quarter of what some of its North European neighbours manage. By 2016 EU law will force Britain to cut down to 22% the 80% of its waste which is currently going into landfill.
3) Packaging contributes to the problem of waste. Designers need to assess how much packaging is actually needed for a product, and how it will be disposed of or recycled.

Audits and Assessments Check Environmental Impact

Industry measures waste, emissions and by-products as part of environmental audits. Life cycle assessments evaluate the environmental impact of a product from design brief to disposal. Every step along the way is examined for environmental friendliness.

Three examples of environmentally friendly design — both to do with laundry:

1) Biological washing powders use enzyme technology to enable them to wash clothes at lower temperatures, producing an energy saving of nearly a third.
2) The latest washing machines have forward-tilting drums which require less water to get the clothes wet — and therefore less energy to heat the water up.
3) Some industrial washing machines have polypropylene drums which are cheaper than using stainless steel, and can be recycled at the end of the drum's life.

Balancing consumer demands against environmental concerns can be difficult. Recycling can be more expensive than using fresh materials and the cost needs to be got back by raising the price of the product. Also some recycled products aren't of such high quality as non-recycled ones.

Landfill sites are the future? — what a load of rubbish...

It's a bit of an eye-opener — only 11% of our rubbish is recycled. It'll make me think twice before I throw away a bottle. But whether you lose sleep over this stuff or not, you still need to learn it.

Why People Buy a Product

If you know what makes people buy things, it becomes easier to design stuff they'll want. So for a designer, finding out this information is dead important.

Good Design and Good Manufacture are Different Things

A well-designed product:

- has the potential to carry out its function really well — because the thinking that's gone into the design is good,
- looks good and attracts consumers.

A well-manufactured product:

- has been made to a good standard — things like the finish, folds, colour and material are all satisfactory,
- is accurate to the original design.

Customers Choose Products for Different Reasons

Not everyone buys a product for the same reasons. People might buy something because of:

COST Customers might think the product is good value for money.

BRAND LOYALTY Customers might be loyal to a company after finding previous goods to be good quality.

AESTHETIC APPEAL Customers might like the look and design of the product.

ADVERTISING This raises product awareness, and can make customers more likely to buy a product.

FASHION Some customers will be more likely to buy something they think is up to date and trendy.

Manufacturers Survey Current Market Trends

It's important for manufacturers to know what consumers think of their product. In order to improve their product they have to keep up with current trends in the market. They have to know:

- what colours, materials and styles are fashionable,
- if consumers like the design and quality of their product,
- if consumers like their advertising,
- how much money consumers are willing to pay for the product.

They do market research to find this stuff out e.g. questionnaires.

Manufacturers also Need Certain Things from a Product

Manufacturers will have opinions on what makes for a 'good' product. Manufacturers often work out a set of criteria stating what they want from a new product. They might require that:

1) the time taken to manufacture and assemble the different parts of the product is reasonably fast,
2) the materials and equipment used to manufacture the product are easy to obtain and cost-effective,
3) the product meets a need — consumers will find it useful,
4) the product carries out its function well — it has been designed and manufactured to a high standard,
5) the product looks good and will be attractive to consumers.

Why buy it? Because it's there...

People are more likely to buy things they want — that's no surprise. But being able to decide what consumers want and why can be worth more money than winning the Lottery. So it's important.

Consumers

What the customer wants or needs drives all design briefs. Without customers, there's no need for the product. If no one buys a manufacturer's products, the manufacturer will go bust.

Customer Satisfaction is what Manufacturers Want

If you just think about design as what you do in lessons, you might see evaluation as the end of the design process. In the world of manufacturing, the end of the process is customer satisfaction...

> Customer satisfaction is achieved when the product works, it's great to use, and it's good value for money. For this to happen, product development, design, production, engineering, marketing and finance all need to work properly together and become a quality system. The key features of a quality system are Quality Control (QC) and Quality Assurance (QA) — see page 67 for more about these.

Consumer Protection keeps us Safe from Dodgy Products

Manufacturers who produce unsafe or unreliable products may be prosecuted under one or more of:

1) The Trade Descriptions Acts ensure that any claims made about a product (e.g. that it is hard-wearing, long-lasting, waterproof) must be true.
2) The Consumer Safety Act legislates over fire regulations and specifications for clothing, toys, electrical goods, etc.
3) The Sale Of Goods Act ensures that products perform as you would expect and that goods last a reasonable length of time.
4) Fire Safety Regulations cover new and second-hand furniture, stuffed furnishings and fabrics, to ensure resistance to ignition and low toxicity fumes.

As well as the law, consumers can get help from:

1. The Office of Fair Trading
2. The British Standards Institution
3. The Environmental Health Department
4. Local Authority Trading Standards Officers
5. Local Authority Consumer Protection Departments

These places give advice on consumer matters:

1. The Citizens' Advice Bureau
2. The Consumers' Advice Council
3. The National Federation of Consumer Groups
4. The National Consumer Council

Products can be Labelled if they Meet certain Standards

1) There are various institutes that set standards of safety, quality or design for certain types of product.
2) Products that meet these standards are usually labelled to show this (see page 31).
3) It's important to meet these standards, as many consumers are more willing to buy 'approved' products.
4) The British Standards Institute (BSI) is one example of this kind of standards institute. Products that meet its standards may display its 'Kitemark' (see page 31).
5) The International Standards Organisation (ISO) also issues certificates to organisations that meet international standards of quality.
6) And if certain products are going to be sold within the European Union (EU), then they have to be 'CE marked'. The CE mark shows that the product has met standards set by the EU.

CE

Other examples of these awarding bodies include:

i) the British Electrotechnical Approvals Board (BEAB),
ii) the British Toy and Hobby Manufacturers' Association (BTMA).

Learn it now or learn it later — that's your consumer choice...

When you're designing and manufacturing, you need to take all this into account. That includes putting all the right labels on and knowing the appropriate laws and safety codes.

Design Considerations

When you're designing your product you may be thinking about that little island in the Bahamas you're going to buy with the profits. But there are some other things you need to consider too...

Trademarks and Patents Stop People Stealing Ideas

1) The aim of using trademarks is to stop people from selling copies of well-known brands. Individuals or companies can register trademarks with the Patent Office.
2) Trademarks are distinctive logos, words or pictures that identify a particular company or product. If someone else then uses your trademark (or something similar), you can sue them.
3) Patents are granted when something new has been invented. They allow the inventor (for a limited time) to stop others from making, using or selling the invention without permission.
4) For a patent to be granted, the invention must involve an 'inventive step' (you won't get a patent for something that's dead obvious), and must be capable of 'industrial application'.

Designs for Mass Production should be Easy to Manufacture

1) Designers have to consider how much time and money is needed to manufacture a design.
2) If products are going to be mass produced in large quantities, it's important that they can be made as quickly and inexpensively as possible.

Designs for mass production should:

- Use materials and components which are easily available.
- Use affordable materials and processes.
- Have an unfussy design, with no unnecessary parts.
- Use standard size components.
- Use standard tools, machinery and equipment, rather than requiring new equipment.
- Use processes which don't require skilled workers.

3) Designing one-off products is a bit different — high quality and individuality are more important and customers are willing to pay more. Therefore, designs can use specialist techniques and equipment, requiring expensive materials and highly-skilled workers.

Products are Designed to be Easy to Maintain

1) It's important that consumers are able to maintain a product in good condition — so that it continues to perform safely and to a high standard.
2) Designers have to consider how a product will be affected by wear and tear, and what maintenance will be needed, *when* they are designing it.
3) Designs can be made easier to maintain by:
   - Designing products to withstand wear and tear, e.g. using strong joints and durable materials.
   - Providing a label or product information leaflet about maintaining the product, e.g. clothes labels.
   - Providing servicing of products to prevent and mend faults, e.g. car maintenance.
   - Making and selling spare parts for the product, e.g. bags for vacuum cleaners.

I have an idea for phones you can, like, carry around...

Don't you dare nick it. That idea is absolutely, definitely MINE.

Labels

Manufacturers are legally obliged to put certain information on packaging, and they're responsible for making sure that it's all true. Anyway, I'll let you get on with the page now...

Manufacturers Must Label their Products Carefully

There are various laws in the UK which describe what information labels on products must give, and protect consumers against dishonest labelling. For example:

1) Trade Descriptions Act (1968) — see page 29,
2) Food Labelling Regulations (1996) — these state what information must be on food packaging,
3) Food Safety Act (1990) — this says that food must be correctly described.

Labels can Give Information about Safety

1) Certain institutes allow manufacturers to label their products with special labels if certain standards have been met (see page 29).
2) Labels also help consumers use and maintain a product.
3) They can give useful safety instructions, such as, *"This way up"*, *"Ensure catch is fully locked before use"* or *"Danger — this part gets hot during use"*.
4) Or they can give maintenance instructions such as, *"Clean with warm water only"*, *"Do not use abrasives"*, *"Oil frequently"* or *"Do not immerse in water"*.

The British Standards Kitemark

Food Labels Have to Tell You Certain Information

The Food Labelling Regulations state that labels on processed foods must give this information:

1) The name of the product and what it is.
2) What ingredients the product contains, in descending order of weight — preservatives, colourants, emulsifiers and other additives must also be listed (but not flavourings).
3) The name and address of the manufacturer, as well as the country of origin of the ingredients (if from a single country).
4) How the product should be stored.
5) The weight or volume of the product.
6) A best-before or use-by date.
7) Instructions for preparation and cooking (if necessary).
8) Whether a product contains genetically modified ingredients (if greater than 1%).

Nutritional Information Sometimes has to be Included

NUTRITIONAL INFORMATION	per 100g	per 55g serving
Energy	2180kJ/525 kcal	1199kJ/289 kcal
Protein	6.5g	3.6g
Carbohydrate	50.0g	27.5g
of which sugars	2.0g	1.1g
Fat	33.0g	18.2g
of which saturates	15.0g	8.3g
Sodium	0.7g	0.4g
Fibre	4.0g	2.2g

- If a special nutritional claim has been made (e.g. 'low sugar') then products must, by law, show the nutritional information.
- This information is often shown in the form of a table.
- It usually shows energy values, protein, carbohydrate, fat, fibre and sodium per 100g and per portion.

Safety Warning: Do not attempt to use this muffin as a parachute...

Although reading this page and learning what's on it may make you want to pull out your own eyeballs, worry not. It's only a page long and once you've learnt it all you can go and take a well-deserved 5-minute break. It's important stuff, so learn it well.

Health and Safety

Safety is essential for the person making the product, and the person using the product. The person making the product is responsible for finding out the hazards, and taking action to minimise the risks.

Wear Protective Clothing while Working...

1) While working, especially with machine tools, make sure your sleeves are rolled back, apron ties are tucked in and if you've got long hair, it's tied back.
2) If material is hot, wear protective gloves, an apron and a face mask.
3) Wear goggles, strong protective gloves or a face mask if using hazardous materials or if a lot of dust or vapours are involved — and make sure there's adequate ventilation.
4) When casting, always wear thick all-body suits, face visors, gauntlets and spats (to protect shoes and feet).

Maybe that's a bit excessive.

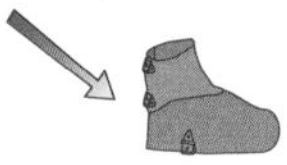

a leather spat

a leather gauntlet

...be Careful with Tools and Machinery...

1) Use the safety guards on lathes and drilling machines.
2) Remove chuck keys from chucks before switching on.
3) Never adjust a machine unless you've switched it off and isolated it first.
4) Never leave machines unattended while switched on.
5) Always secure work safely — e.g. you should clamp work securely for drilling.
6) Don't use machines or hand tools unless you have been shown how.
7) Ensure that any dust extraction equipment is connected and working properly.
8) Be careful when carrying heavy or large materials — lift things properly.
9) Never operate machines unless allowed to, and under supervision where appropriate.
10) Know where the EMERGENCY STOP buttons are to switch off and isolate a machine (but only use them when needed).

Chucks and Chuck Keys...
A chuck key is one of those things you use to tighten a drill bit holder (a chuck). You get chucks on various tools.

...Handle Materials and Waste Sensibly...

1) Choose your materials sensibly (only use hazardous materials where necessary).
2) Make sure materials are safe to handle. Deburr metal (file down any rough edges) before you start work. (And if metal is greased, degrease it first.)
3) Beware of naked flames or red-hot heating elements — and keep them away from flammable liquids.
4) Make sure you dispose of waste properly.
5) When storing material, make sure it's put away safely so it can't fall or slide and injure anyone.
6) Never clear away metal shavings/dust with your bare hands — use the brush provided.

...basically, just don't be a Moron

1) Don't run or move quickly around the workshop.
2) Never throw anything across the workshop.
3) Be tidy — put tools away when not in use.
4) Report any accidents, faults, spillages or breakages to your teacher immediately.
5) Speak up if you see someone else behaving dangerously in the workshop.

Learn this page — it'll help you avoid horrific injury...

Blimey, that's a lot of stuff to learn. Safety rules are common sense, but you've got to learn them.

Health and Safety

Safety is also important for the consumer.
People don't want to risk death every time they boil the kettle.

Design Safe Products — Think About the Consumer

When designing products, think 'safety'. Products which may harm the end user are generally inappropriate. Sometimes it's impossible to avoid potential harm completely (e.g. sharp tools), but for these products effort should be made to at least minimise the risks.

1) Toys and tools should have unnecessary sharp corners and edges smoothed so that consumers can't cut themselves. (This includes any attachments — e.g. attaching the eyes of a teddy bear by 10 cm metal spikes would be a thoroughly bad and unsafe idea.)
2) Toys often end up in children's mouths, so don't finish the surface with any toxic paint or varnish.
3) Small components must be firmly attached so that a young child can't pull them off — this would be a choking hazard.
4) Use standard components wherever you can, because these have already been rigorously tested by the manufacturer — this helps make sure that safety standards are met.

There are Laws on Safety

To protect consumers, there are safety standards applied to many products by the British Standards Institute (BSI). Products which meet these standards are awarded the Kitemark (see p31). Manufacturers usually incorporate this in their label. Many plastic products have it moulded on.

The Health and Safety at Work Act and COSHH (Control Of Substances Hazardous to Health) relate to safety in the workplace. They're designed to protect you from hazardous (mainly chemical) products or dangerous working practices which may pose a risk to your health.

Risk Assessment is Important for Workers and Consumers

Risk assessment is a procedure which is carried out to identify and minimise any potential risks of using chemicals, machinery or equipment. It may also be carried out on a product to highlight any potential risk to the end user and ensure precautions are taken to minimise potential danger.

Employers, workshop managers and your technology teacher must assess the risks involved in using workshop facilities and justify the level of precaution taken, e.g. placing warning or caution signs on machines, installing non-slip flooring or erecting barriers and guards.

Choose a piece of machinery you use in school and ask yourself these questions:

1) What could go wrong?
2) What effect would this have?
3) What can I do to prevent it happening?
4) What system could I implement to make sure the risk is minimised?

You'll never pass the course if your product kills people...

Risk assessment comes down to working out what might go horribly wrong and finding the best way to prevent it going horribly wrong. Toys are a good example of safety in design — kids put things in their mouths, and you don't want them to choke or poison themselves.

Choosing the Best Material to Use

Selecting the right materials isn't easy. But it's something you've got to be able to do, otherwise you can end up in a right pickle.

Different Factors affect your Selection of Material

You should be able to make a good choice as long as you understand a material's properties, and know what it's being used for.

Functional Requirements — What does the product have to do?

Ask yourself the following questions:

1) What demands will be made on the material? (Will it have to withstand heavy loads or chemicals? Will it have to conduct heat or electricity?)
2) Will it be for outdoor or indoor use? (If it's for outside, you'll need to consider whether your material will corrode.)
3) Does it need to fit in with an environment? (Your material might need to be a particular style or have a certain look.)

Most of this car seems to have rusted away, leaving just the boot and half the back wheel. Probably the result of a poor choice of material.

Economics — How much money have you got?

You'll need to consider the following points:

1) The size of the product — materials like pewter are expensive, but may be a good choice for a small item of jewellery.
2) Scale of production — is your product a one-off, or will it be batch or mass produced? Stainless steel could be a possible material for a one-off product. But if you're mass-producing something that would be equally as good made from some kind of plastic, that might be cheaper.

Availability of Supply — What can you get hold of?

Can you get hold of the material you want? And if you can, can you get it in a suitable form? Most materials are only available in standard forms and sizes, and it can be very expensive to get a material in any other form. This will have a direct effect on the cost and the method of manufacture.

For example, materials might be available as granules, strips, bars, tubes, rough sawn, planed...

Manufacturing Method — How will the product be made?

1) Some materials are easier to join than others (which will affect the production method used).
2) Also, the material must be suitable for the intended production method (and vice versa). For example, you can make something out of certain plastics using injection moulding, but it's no good planning to use this technique for wood.

I reckon you should just make everything out of cheese...

You need to know about different materials so you can choose the right one for the job in hand. Don't make a fireguard or teapot from chocolate, for example — they won't be much use. It sounds obvious, but it's a mistake that amateurs make all too often. Be smart — don't be one of them.

Revision Summary

You can't go just yet. Oh no. You have to do these little questions first, to check you've learnt everything in this section. Think of it as Learning Quality Control.

1) What is 'market pull'? Give an example of where it has influenced design.
2) What is 'technological push'? Give an example of where it has influenced design.
3) Give an example of how nature has inspired the function of a product.
4) Give an example of how nature has inspired the aesthetics of a product.
5) What is the Fibonacci Series?
6) Why do you need to do product analysis?
7) What are form and function?
8) Name five other factors that you should look at when analysing a product.
9) Should a designer care about the safety of manufacturing workers?
10) If you were being environmentally responsible, what kind of material might you choose for a disposable product?
11) What is ergonomics?
12) What's the fancy name for body measurement data?
13) What sort of impact can a badly designed product have on the user's health?
14) Name two non-renewable resources.
15) Give three examples of ways that manufacturers and designers can reduce the environmental impact of a product.
16) Explain the difference between good design and good manufacture.
17) Give five reasons why a consumer might choose a particular product.
18) What are the Trade Descriptions Acts about?
19) What is the Sale of Goods Act for?
20) Explain why many companies like to get their products approved by an institute like the BSI or ISO. What does the CE mark signify?
21) What is a patent? What kind of thing can be awarded a patent?
22) Give five ways in which a design can be made more suitable for mass production.
23) Give four ways in which a design can be made easier to maintain.
24) Whose symbol is the Kitemark? What do they do?
25) Give an example of a maintenance/safety label that you might see on a hand-held electric blender.
26) If you see someone breaking safety rules in the workshop, what should you do?
27) When should you wear goggles? (In the context of Product Design.)
28) Why are small removable parts inappropriate to use on toys for very small children?
29) Why must surface treatments on toys be non-toxic?
30) What is risk assessment? Who does it?
31) Describe four different factors which should affect your selection of material for a product.

Paper and Board

There are loads of different types of paper and board — each designed to suit a particular situation.

Paper — Ones You Need to Know About and Use

1) Cartridge paper has a textured surface, which is great for sketching with pencils, crayons, pastels, gouache, inks and watercolours.
2) Layout paper is thin and translucent (you can see light through it) and is used for general design work — particularly generating ideas.
3) Bleed-proof paper is used by designers when drawing with felt-tips and marker pens. The ink doesn't spread out (bleed) — it stays put.
4) Tracing paper is translucent, and is used to copy images.
5) Photocopy paper is probably the paper you use most in class. It's most commonly used in either A4 or A3 sizes. It's cheap.
6) Grid paper may have a square, isometric or perspective pre-printed pattern on it — square grid paper is useful for orthographic drawings and nets (for product developments), and isometric grid paper is good for presentation drawings.

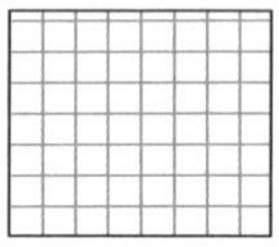
square grid paper

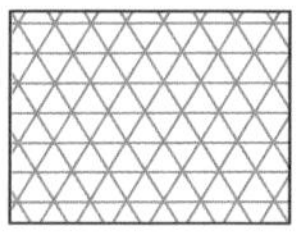
isometric grid paper

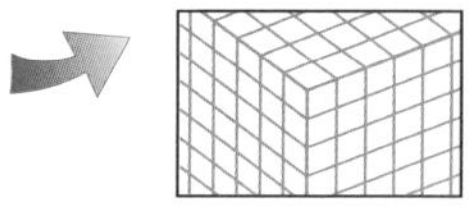
perspective grid paper

Board — These are the Ones you Need to Know About

The weight of paper and card is measured in gsm (grams per square metre). Above 200 gsm, it's not paper any more — it's board.

1) Mounting card is used to mount drawings and photographs for presentation, or for framing — usually by cutting a 'window'.
2) Foamboard (polystyrene foam laminated between card) is lightweight. Used for models and mounting.
3) Solid white board has a high quality bleached surface, which is ideal for printing, and is used loads in primary packaging, i.e. the packaging that's used for individual items (as opposed to secondary packaging, which might be a big box used to transport lots of the same item to shops, etc.).
4) Corrugated card is used a lot in secondary packaging to protect products during transit. It's made up of a fluted inner core sandwiched between two outer layers.
5) Duplex board has a different colour and texture on each side. It's often used where only one surface is seen, so that only one side needs to be smooth for printing. It's unbleached, so it's ideal for food packaging.
6) Klett is a type of corrugated board used in packaging which uses double-sided tape instead of cow gum to bond it together.

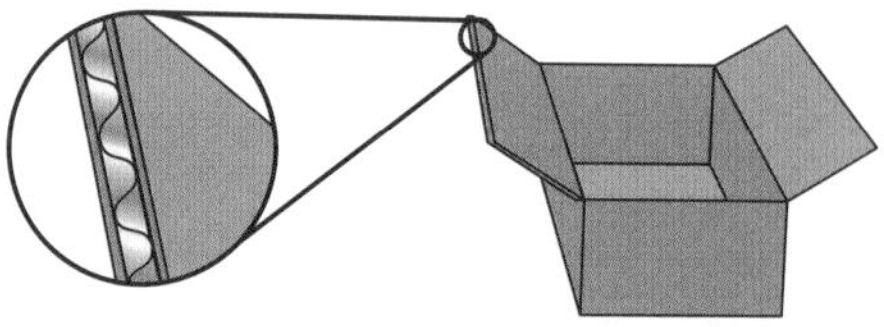
corrugated cardboard

Yes, cow gum. As in "made from boiled up cows."

Board is Often Made from Recycled Paper

1) As paper and card are made from wood pulp, most of it's recyclable and from sustainable resources.
2) It's therefore environmentally friendly.
3) A lot of cardboard is made from recycled material.

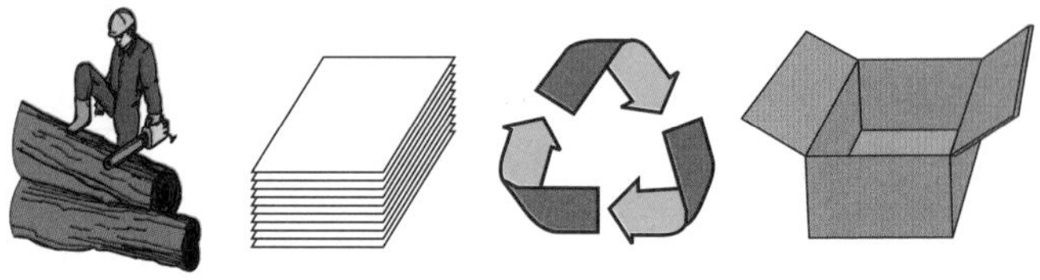

Paper and board — I can't handle the excitement...

Well there it is... a big fat page on paper and board. I don't blame you if you're feeling a bit "bored". Ha ha, geddit? Anyway, stop moaning — revision isn't about fun. That's why we have Ant and Dec.

Wood

Woods can be divided into two main categories — softwood and hardwood.
This is not a description of the wood — it just means what type of tree it comes from.

Softwood — Evergreen Trees, like Pine

1) Most softwood trees are coniferous (cone bearing). They typically have thin, needle-like leaves and are evergreen — e.g. pine, cedar and yew.
2) They grow in colder climates and are fast growing — most reaching maturity within 30 years. This makes them easy to replace with new trees, so they're usually cheaper than hardwoods.

Pines:

1) There are several types of pine but they're all generally pale yellow with brown streaks.
2) Scots pine is fairly strong but knotty.
3) Parana pine is more expensive — it's hard and is best used for interior joinery.

Pine trees — before and after the 'chop'.

Hardwood — Deciduous Trees, like Oak

1) Most hardwood trees are broadleaved and deciduous (they shed their leaves annually) — e.g. oak, mahogany, beech and elm.
2) Broadleaf trees grow in warm climates and are usually slow growing. They can take around a hundred years to mature, so they're generally more expensive than softwoods.

Colours of the common hardwoods:

mahogany	reddish brown	elm	light reddish brown
beech	creamy/pinkish	oak	rich light brown

A deciduous tree in autumn. Ah, innit pretty...

The Bit about Woodstain...

Most woods need protection, particularly if they're going to be used outdoors.
Most hardwoods have an attractive grain and often don't have paint as a surface finish.

1) Polyurethane varnish can be used to seal and protect the surface of the wood, and give it a smooth surface finish. You can buy it clear or in a wide range of colours.
2) Woodstain can be applied to wood to enhance the appearance of the wood's grain. It's available in natural colours but also in bright blues, reds etc. Stains usually don't protect the wood, so varnish may need to be applied afterwards.
3) Oil can be used to maintain a natural appearance of the wood. Some oil-based finishes also offer protection to wood used outdoors.
4) Paint is often used to colour and protect wood. Emulsion paints are cheap, but they are water-based, so they don't protect wood from water. Polyurethane paint is more expensive but is waterproof and much tougher.

I wood have put two pages in on this if I could...

Ah... wood's lovely, isn't it. Except for the splinters. Or 'spelks', as my friend Tim would have it. If he got splinters, he'd say, *"Ayaz — spelks!"* (That's just how they talk in my part of the world.)

Manufactured Boards

Solid woods are cut straight from the tree. Man-made woods (boards) are made from the bits of waste that are produced when the trunks and branches are cut into planks.

Plywood — Loads of Layers

Plywood is a very popular man-made board, used for building and general construction.

1) Plywood is very strong for its weight and thickness, compared with solid wood.
2) It's made up of several layers — always an odd number of them.
3) The layers are glued with their grain at 90 degrees to each other — which is why it's so strong.
4) The outside of the board can be finished with a nice veneer (a thin layer of good quality wood) to make it look better.

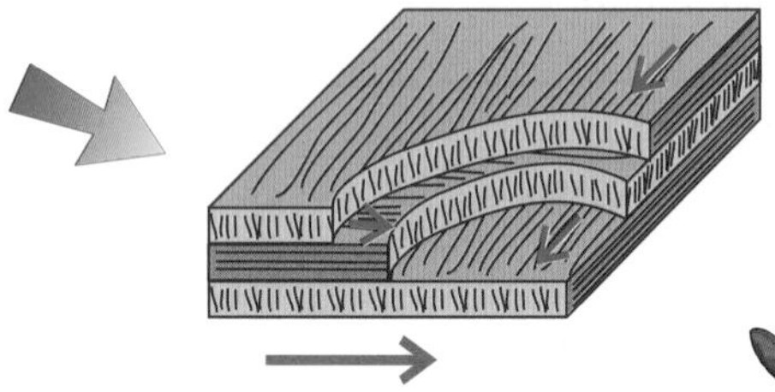

Blockboard and Laminboard — Blocks in a 'Sandwich'

Blockboard and laminboard are boards of similar construction. Although not as strong as plywood, they're a cheap substitute, especially when thicker boards are required.

1) Strips of softwood are glued together, side by side, and sandwiched between two veneers. The veneers add strength and make the board look nicer.
2) The outer veneers are glued with their grain at right angles to the grain of the inner core — this makes the board stronger.
3) The softwood used is usually pine or spruce. (Some countries use hardwood instead.)
4) The width of the softwood for laminboard is between 5 mm and 7 mm.
5) The width of the softwood for blockboard is thicker, at between 7 mm and 25 mm.

MDF and Chipboard — MFI eat your heart out...

Medium Density Fibreboard

1) Medium density fibreboard (MDF) is a popular board that's very cost-effective (cheap).
2) MDF has smooth faces and takes paint and other finishes well.

I reckon this desk is made with painted MDF.

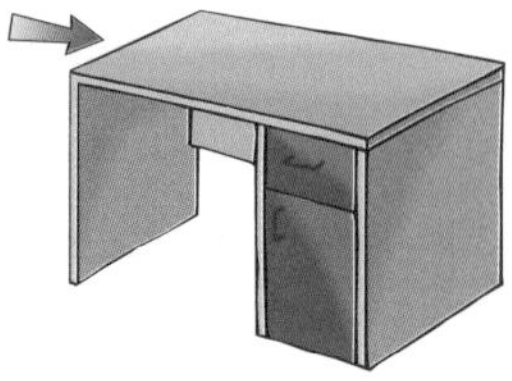

Chipboard

1) This is produced by compressing wood particles together with glue.
2) It's cheap but not very strong, so is usually used with a hardwood or plastic veneered surface in cheap furniture.

A little bit of chipboard.

"Enjoying learning about wood?" — "No, I'm board"...

Man-made boards are available in large sizes — because they're not restricted by the size of the tree, like solid wood is. Knock-down (KD) joints (see p57) are the easiest way to join these boards.

Metals

Some metals are pure metals and others (alloys) are mixtures of different metals.
Both types of metal can be classified into two basic groups — ferrous and non-ferrous.

Ferrous Metals contain Iron

1) These are the metals that contain iron.
2) Because of this, almost all of them are magnetic.
3) Examples: mild steel
   high-carbon steel
   stainless steel

METAL	PROPERTIES	USES
MILD STEEL	Quite strong and cheap but rusts easily and can't be hardened or tempered.	car bodies, screws, nuts, bolts, nails, washing machines
HIGH-CARBON STEEL	Harder than mild steel and can be hardened and tempered. But it's not as easy to work and also rusts.	drills, files, chisels, saws
STAINLESS STEEL	Hard and won't rust, but is more expensive.	medical equipment, sinks, kettles, cutlery (e.g. knives)

Non-Ferrous Metals — guess what? — Don't contain Iron

1) If a metal doesn't contain iron, it's non-ferrous.
2) Examples: aluminium
   brass
   copper

METAL	PROPERTIES	USES
ALUMINIUM	Lightweight and corrosion-resistant but expensive and not as strong as steel	aeroplanes, cans, ladders
BRASS	Quite strong, corrosion-resistant, malleable, ductile and looks good	door handles, electrical parts
COPPER	Relatively soft, malleable and ductile and a very good electrical conductor	wiring, pipes

An Alloy is a Mixture, e.g. Brass = Copper + Zinc

1) An alloy is a mixture of two or more metals, or a metal mixed with another element.
2) An alloy is a new material with different properties and different working characteristics.
3) Alloys can be grouped as ferrous *(contains iron), e.g. steel = iron + carbon*, and non-ferrous *(doesn't contain iron), e.g. brass = copper + zinc*.

Different types of steel also contain varying quantities of other metals, such as chromium.

You can Buy Metals in Loads of Shapes and Sizes

1) Metal is extracted from the earth in the form of metal ore. It's then refined and processed to produce usable materials.
2) Metals are commonly available in a wide range of shapes and sizes, because it can be very difficult to convert one shape to another.

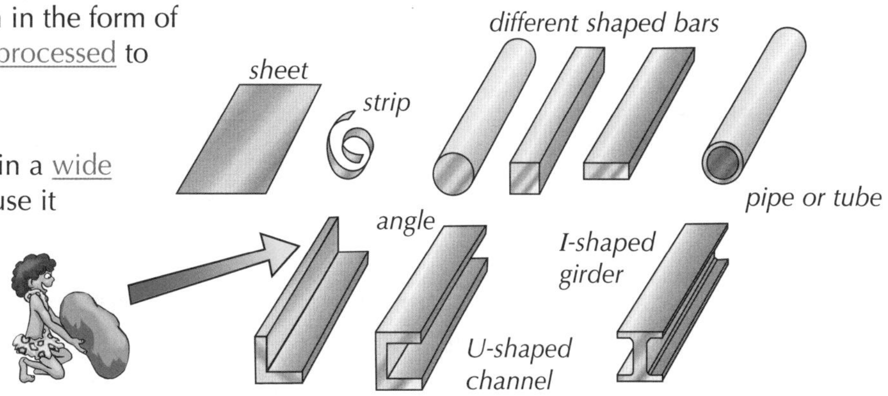

Metals — hahahaha...

All those metals — not confusing at all. Learn the ferrous metals, non-ferrous metals and alloys.

Metals

Metals are rarely used in their raw form without treating them first. Most need some kind of surface finish — either for aesthetic (appearance) reasons or to provide protection.

Heat Treatments — for Softening or Toughening

Metals can be heat-treated to change their properties and characteristics. The three main types of treatment are listed below:

1) Annealing — softening metal by heating and leaving to cool.
2) Hardening — heating and rapidly cooling a metal. The metal is heated to its upper critical temperature then plunged into cold water. It leaves the metal brittle, so is often followed by a process known as tempering...
3) Tempering — to make the metal tougher and less likely to break.

At the upper critical temperature, the atoms in the metal 'rearrange themselves' into a different structure.

When steel is tempered, it's first cleaned to make it bright in appearance and then gently heated. As it gets hotter, it changes gradually from a pale straw colour to blue — and the colour shows you how tough it's become.

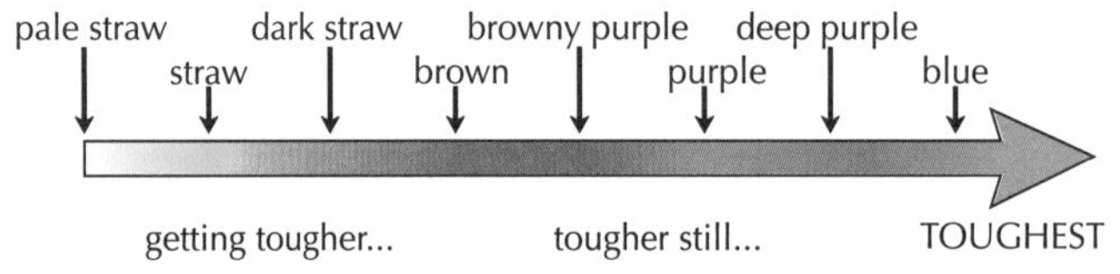

Tempering of Steel

Surface Finishes — for Protection and Looks

1) Painting

A primer such as red oxide or zinc chromate is needed for steel (to form a chemical bond with the metal surface). Hammerite is a durable top coat that's available in a range of colours and finishes — it offers protection and is quick drying.

2) Plastic coating

A metal is heated evenly in an oven and then plunged into fluidised powder (i.e. very fine powder that's made to act like a liquid by passing air through it during the process of dipping) for a few seconds. The metal, with this thin coating of plastic, is then returned to the oven to completely fuse it to the surface.

3) Polishing

This may be carried out by hand or by using a buffing wheel. The wheel is coated with abrasive polish and the metal is held against the spinning wheel until the required surface finish is achieved.

4) Lacquering

This provides a barrier against tarnishing and oxidising, and is often used on decorative items such as jewellery. A thin layer of cellulose, gum or varnish is applied to leave a transparent coating.

Heat treatment? — sounds like the hairdresser's...

The metal must be thoroughly cleaned (e.g. with paraffin or white spirit) before adding a finish. You wouldn't want that Hammerite peeling off now would you — what a disaster that'd be.

Plastics

Most plastics are produced by industry using water, oil (or coal or gas), air and salt.
There are two families of plastics — thermoplastics and thermosetting plastics.

Thermoplastics — Recyclable and Bendy

Please re-use or recycle this bag.

1) Thermoplastics are recyclable. They're also easily formed into shapes.
2) They don't resist heat very well, so they can be ground down, melted and re-used — very important in today's society of increasing waste.
3) A moulded shape can be reheated and it will return to its original state — the material is known as having plastic memory.
4) Examples of thermoplastics: acrylic, ABS, polystyrene and polyethylene (polythene).

Thermosetting Plastics — Non-Recyclable and (usually) Rigid

1) These types of plastic are non-recyclable.
2) They resist heat and fire so are often used for electrical fittings and pan handles.
3) These types of plastic undergo a chemical change when heated (unlike thermoplastics) to become hard and rigid. They're not used in schools very often.
4) Examples of thermosetting plastics: melamine-formaldehyde, polyester resin, epoxy resin and urea-formaldehyde.

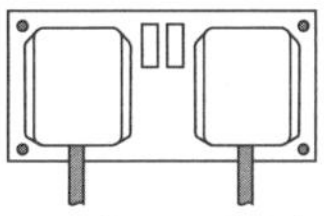
urea-formaldehyde

melamine-formaldehyde

...an' ye can get 'em in loads of different forms...

1) Plastics can be bought in many different forms — from powders, granules, pellets and liquids (for processing into finished products), through to films, sheets, rods, tubes and extruded mouldings (complex shapes).
2) Plastics don't need protective surface finishes, due to high resistance to corrosion and decay.
3) But for a nice appearance, wet and dry paper (silicon carbide paper) is applied to remove scratches from the plastic, and followed up with a mild abrasive polish or anti-static cream.
4) Alternatively, a buffing machine can be used. No Spike jokes, please.

New Plastics are still being Developed

The following materials are fairly recently-developed and have loads of uses:

1) Plastizote is a closed-cell polyethylene foam that has eliminated the need for the toxic chemicals currently used in the foam industry. It's suitable for a wide range of products, including shoe insoles, buoyancy aids and reusable packaging.
2) Plastics that conduct electricity can be made by putting stainless steel fibres into plastics.

Life in plastic — it's fantastic...

Thermosetting plastics can't be remoulded — i.e. once they're set, they're set permanently.
Like when you pull a funny face and the wind changes. Something like that, anyway.

Composites and Smart Materials

Composites and 'smart materials' have allowed new types of product to be made.

Composites — Improved Properties through Bonding...

Composite materials are formed from two or more materials bonded together.

1) When two or more materials are combined by bonding, a composite material is formed.
2) Mechanical and other properties are improved, resulting in excellent strength-to-weight ratios in the majority of composites.
3) Tufnol is an example of a composite: woven linen is impregnated with a phenolic resin. This can then be used in gears, bearings etc.

Plastic can be Reinforced with Glass or Carbon Fibres

Glass-Reinforced Plastic (GRP)

1) Glass-Reinforced Plastic (GRP) is a popular choice for large structural items such as boats and car bodies.
2) This reinforced plastic has glass fibre strands that give greater strength to the material.
3) The glass fibre is available as woven fabric, matting and loose strands.

Carbon Fibre

1) This is similar to GRP, but instead of glass fibres, carbon fibres are used. This makes the material much stronger.
2) As well as being mechanically stronger, the material is also lighter in weight.
3) Products made from carbon-fibre composites include protective helmets, bulletproof vests and racing cars.

'Smart' Materials have Clever Properties

Nitinol

1) Nitinol is a 'shape memory alloy', and is an example of a so-called 'smart material'.
2) It can be easily shaped when cool, but returns to a 'remembered' shape when heated above a certain temperature.
3) So if your glasses are made of this and you accidentally bend them, you can just pop them into a bowl of hot water and they'll jump back into shape.

Silicon

1) Silicon is a semiconductor, meaning its resistance decreases as its temperature increases.
2) Single crystals of silicon are cut into thin wafers and have transistors (and other circuit elements) etched onto the surface. A large chip of 20 cm diameter can contain up to one thousand million circuit elements.
3) Computers have their Central Processing Unit (CPU) made from a single integrated circuit (chip).

It's amazing what a bit of bonding can do...

Shape memory alloys sound great. You can even get a 'magic spoon' that jumps into a different shape as soon as you put it in hot tea. Just one of the ways in which technology changes lives.

Ceramics

A whole, beautiful page about pots. Don't scoff. Pots are very interesting and important... ish.

Ceramic Products are Often Made Using Clay

1) The materials used to make ceramics are non-metallic, inorganic compounds, usually oxides but also nitrides, borides, carbides and silicides.
2) One of the main materials used to make ceramics is clay — a type of soil which is malleable when moist and can be hardened by heating it to high temperatures (firing).
3) Clays are dug from the ground (they're formed by the weathering of rocks like granite). They're often dried and crushed, and then mixed with other minerals and water to make them more workable. It is sold by weight.
4) Moist, unhardened clay is called 'body clay'. Watered down clay (used to help stick bits of clay together) is called 'slip'.

How Clay Pottery is Made

- Body clay can be moulded into shape by hand, or by using a potter's wheel. Liquid clay can be poured into moulds.
- The clay is then air dried before being heated to high temperatures (usually over 1000°C) to harden it. It is often heated in a specialised oven called a kiln.
- Glazes are sometimes applied before firing. They are made up of glass, stiffeners and melting agents. The glaze melts during firing and then hardens to give the pottery an attractive finish.

There are Different Types of Clay

Earthenware clays — cheap and easily available. Used for tiles, sewer pipes, pots and sometimes tableware.

Stoneware clays — better quality clay. Used for tableware. Often glazed to improve its looks.

Porcelain — made from white, China clay. Good quality, used for ornaments and posh tableware.

Not all ceramics are made from clay. Other materials such as Plaster of Paris (a white powder that sets when mixed with water) are also used.

Ceramics are Used for More than Just Pottery

1) Ceramics can resist high temperatures without melting. This means they are used as one of the materials in heat-shield tiles and nose-cones on space shuttles.
2) They are also used for some of the components in light bulbs and spark plugs because of their resistance to heat.
3) Ceramic particles of iron oxide are used in magnetic recording media, e.g. tapes, disks.
4) New ceramic materials are being developed with useful properties, e.g. copper-oxide-based ceramics which become superconductive at high temperatures.

Harry Potter and the Flight of the Big Stoneware Pot...

Easy page this. Lots of important exam-grade information cunningly disguised as some doddery waffle about pottery. But don't think you can get away without learning it...

Textiles

Fibres are the raw material of textiles, e.g. wool off the sheep's back. Yarns are fibres which have been twisted or spun into a thread. And fabric is sheets of material made from yarn or bonded fibres.

Fibres can be Natural or Man-made

Natural Fibres

1) Animal — wool from animals, e.g. sheep, alpaca, angora goats and Kashmir goats.
2) Vegetable — fibres from plants, e.g. linen, cotton, hessian.

Man-made Fibres

1) Regenerated — natural fibres that have been industrially processed, e.g. viscose, acetate.
2) Synthetic — fibres completely man-made using chemicals, e.g. nylon, polyester, acrylic, elastane.

Fabric can be Woven, Knitted or Bonded

Materials are constructed in different ways:

1) Woven fabrics are two sets of yarns (called the warp and the weft) weaved under and over each other to create a fabric. Types of weave include plain weave and twill weave.
2) Knitted fabrics are yarns knitted together using needles or a knitting machine.
3) Non-woven fabrics are created by bonding or felting fibres together.

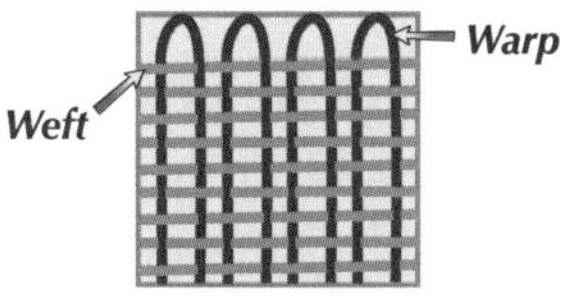

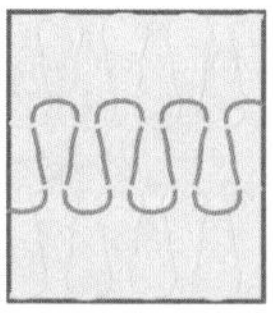

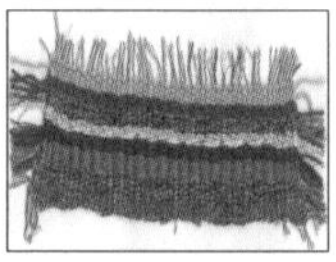

Weaving

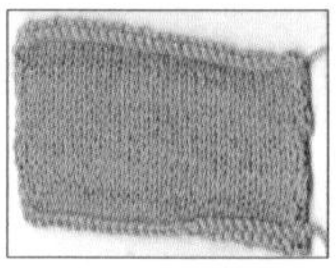

Knitting

Different Fabrics have Different Properties

The properties of materials are the way they behave, look and feel.

Material	Uses	Properties include:
Cotton	clothes, sheets, tablecloths	durable, absorbent, strong
Wool	jumpers, blankets, hats	warm, absorbent, flammable
Nylon	tents, raincoats, backpacks	strong, durable, machine-washable
Lycra	sportswear, socks, belts	elastic, soft, lightweight

Many fabrics are composites — they combine different fibres in one fabric, e.g. cotton and lycra. This means they combine the properties of different fibres, e.g. absorbent and stretchy.

These Components are often used in Textile Products...

buttons

zips

threads

No shock, Sherlock...

Dot Cotton — the fabric of society...

Yarn is sold by weight (grams) and ply (two-ply, three-ply etc.) Fabrics are sold on rolls, or by the yard. Fascinating stuff this. I promise on my free Gideon Bible that you need to know it.

Food

There are five nutrients that are vital to health — proteins, fats, carbohydrates, vitamins and minerals.

You can Classify Food Materials into Five Groups

Carbohydrates

1) Carbohydrates provide the body with energy.
2) They can be classified into two groups — sugars and starches.
3) Sources of sugars include full sugar drinks, biscuits and cakes.
4) Sources of starch include bread, pasta and potatoes.

Protein

1) Protein is needed by the body to grow new cells. Protein is also needed to repair old and damaged cells.
2) Animal sources include meat, fish, cheese and eggs.
   Vegetable sources include lentils, peas, beans and nuts.

Fat

1) Fat supplies the body with a concentrated energy source and with fat-soluble vitamins (A, D, E and K).
2) BUT — too much fat in our diet has been linked to obesity (being overweight) and heart disease.
3) Animal sources include butter and lard (visible fats), cakes and pastries (invisible fats).
   Vegetable sources include olives, olive oil, sunflower oil and avocados.

Vitamins

Vitamins help other nutrients to work and can prevent some diseases. E.g.

- Vitamin A is needed for good eyesight, growth and functions of tissues.
  Sources include: liver, butter, eggs, fish oils.
- Vitamin D aids the absorption of calcium.
  Sources include: fatty fish and eggs.

Minerals

Minerals also help other nutrients to work and help keep you healthy. E.g.

- Calcium, needed for strong bones and teeth.
  Sources include: milk products, tofu, salmon, white bread and hard water.
- Iron, needed to form part of red blood cells.
  Sources include: dark green vegetables and meat.

Some Food Materials have Useful Characteristics

1) Protein Foods (things like eggs, nuts, meat and cheese)Eggs are great for loads of reasons —

Eggs set (coagulate) when heated, which gives strength to a product.

Eggs can be added to sauces to help thicken them when heated gently.

Egg whites can be whisked to create a foam, which makes products light and fluffy.

Egg yolk contains an emulsifier (lecithin), which holds oil and water together when they want to pull apart, e.g. in mayonnaise.

2) Carbohydrate Foods

Flour — a starchy carbohydrate

- Flour adds texture and structure.
- Flour can be used to thicken sauces (gelatinisation) by absorbing the liquid in the sauce and making a gel.

Sugary carbohydrates

- Sugary carbohydrates sweeten foods.
- Sugary carbohydrates caramelise with heat to thicken food and add flavour.

Fibre

- Fibre found in carbohydrate foods helps to give products bulk.
- Fibre absorbs liquid added to the product and makes it bigger and easier to digest.

3) Fatty Foods

- Fatty foods in general add flavour, colour and texture to dishes.
- Butter gives pastry a nice flavour and lard helps to shorten the pastry (by surrounding the flour particles) — this gives the pastry a nice crumbly texture.

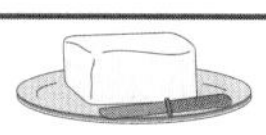

There's a couple of other things you need to know...

1) Food is measured in weight (grams and kilograms) or volume (litres).
2) Food is sold in lots of different forms, e.g. frozen, fresh, canned, liquid, dehydrated.

For a bit of revision you can go down to your local market and buy loads of yummy stuff...

Electrical Components

If you want to make a fancy design with moving parts and buzzers and lights, then you need to get your head round these two pages. The wonder. The mystery. The systems.

A System has an Input, a Process and an Output

Input → Process → Output

1) The input is a signal that starts the system off.
2) The process is what happens to the input to change it into an output. Information from the input controls the output.
3) The output is the result of the system.

Inputs of Electrical Systems Include Switches and Sensors

INPUT DEVICE	CIRCUIT SYMBOL	LOOKS LIKE	FUNCTION	POSSIBLE USES
switch	open  closed 		They complete electric circuits, allowing current to flow around them.	light switches, 'on' buttons of various electrical products
thermistor (temperature sensor)	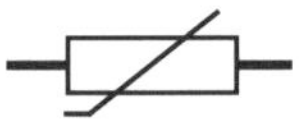		Resistance falls in hot conditions, allowing current to flow around circuit.	thermostats for central heating, temperature detectors in car engines
light-dependent resistor (senses light)	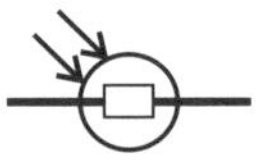	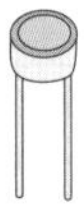	Resistance falls in light, allowing current to flow around circuit.	burglar detectors

Outputs of Electrical Systems Include Lamps and Buzzers

OUTPUT DEVICE	CIRCUIT SYMBOL	LOOKS LIKE	FUNCTION	POSSIBLE USES
lamp	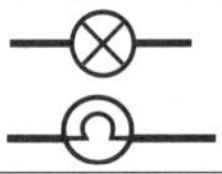 or		Converts electrical energy into light.	toys, security lights, shop displays
buzzer			Converts electrical energy into sound.	alarms, toys
motor			Converts electrical energy into rotary motion.	powering mechanisms, turning objects e.g. wheels on toy car
LED (light-emitting diode)	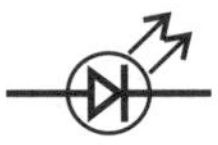		Gives out light, only lets current go in one direction.	used in circuits to indicate when they are working
solenoid			Converts electrical energy into small linear movements	locks, toys

Blame Edison for this page*...

And finally, that useful little source of energy: the battery.

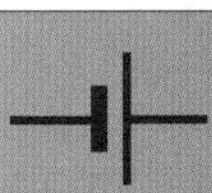

* If you were living in the Neolithic period, all you'd have to revise is how to make a simple stone axe. Darn the progress of civilisation.

Mechanisms

There are lots of simple mechanisms you can use. Some are better for 2D items (e.g. linkages in pop-up cards) and some for 3D things (e.g. cams in mechanical toys). But they're all smashing.

There are Four Types of Motion used in Mechanical Systems

1) Linear Motion — moving in a straight line in one direction, e.g. a rocket.
2) Rotary Motion — moving in a circle, e.g. a drill.
3) Oscillating Motion — moving backwards and forwards in an arc, e.g. a swing.
4) Reciprocating Motion — moving backwards and forwards in a straight line, e.g. a bicycle pump.

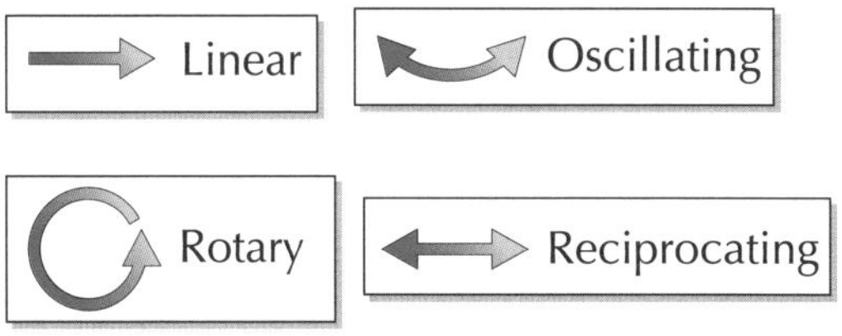

Mechanical Systems Transfer Motion and Force

1) Mechanical systems change an input motion and force into an output motion and force.
2) They can make a motion and force bigger or smaller. They can also change the direction of a motion and force, or change one type of motion into another. Clever things.
3) Mechanical systems are designed to make things easier for you to do — they give you 'mechanical advantage'. Simple mechanisms you might use in your designs include:

Gears

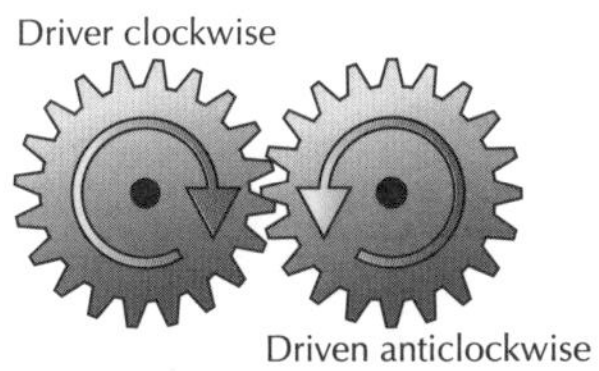

1) Gears are toothed wheels which interlock. They transfer rotary motion.

Linkages

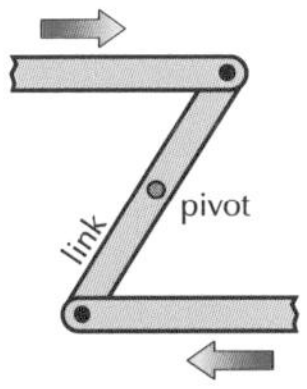

2) Linkages connect different parts of a mechanism. They can transfer forces and change the direction of motion.

Levers

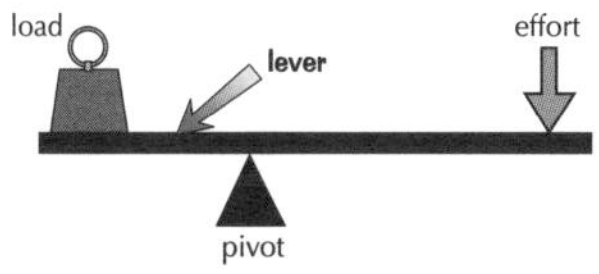

3) Levers enable an object to be lifted with less effort. As you move the pivot closer to the load it becomes easier to lift.

Cams

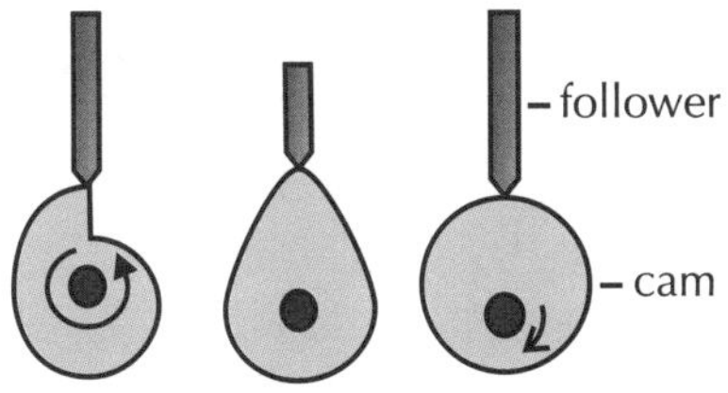

4) Cams change rotary motion into reciprocating motion. The cam mechanism is made up of a rotating shape and a "follower" which follows the shape of the cam.

Cranks

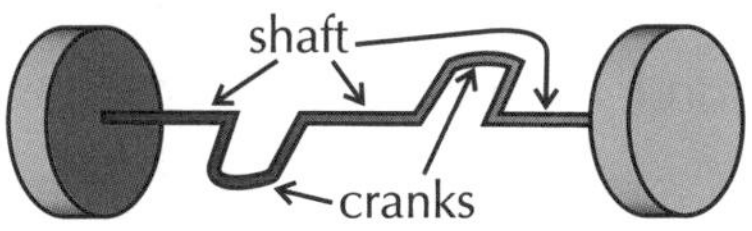

5) Cranks can be as simple as a handle on a shaft. As you increase the distance between the handle and the shaft it becomes easier to turn — cranks give you mechanical advantage.

Pulleys

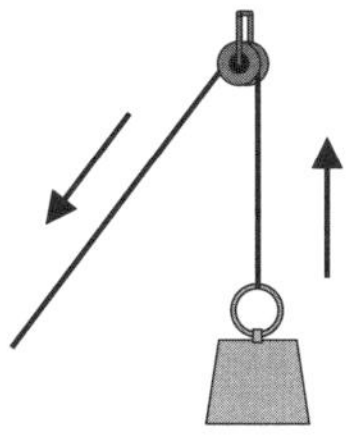

6) Pulleys change the direction of the force needed to lift a load — you can lift the load by pulling, rather than pushing.

Uplifting jumper — or woolly pulley...

Force is just the thump, push, pull, shove, whack, gravity... the strength and power that are acting on an object. The force Yoda is banging on about in Star Wars is a whole different kettle of fish.

Revision Summary

Don't you just love materials? Wood, plastic, metal, textiles, ceramics.... their names shall go down in history as good, solid kinds of stuff that you could make things out of. And you need to learn about THEM ALL. Even those pesky electronic components. Every single one. Or I'll come round to your gran's house and kill her tomato plants. Honest.

1) In what units are the weights of paper and card measured?
2) Describe duplex board, and say why it's used for food packaging.
3) What is Klett?
4) Name three types of softwood and three types of hardwood.
5) What does 'deciduous' mean?
6) Describe two different types of paint you can use on wood.
7) Why is plywood so strong?
8) How is blockboard made?
9) What do all ferrous metals contain?
10) Name three non-ferrous metals.
11) Name a ferrous alloy, and the two metals it is made from.
12) Describe the process of tempering steel.
13) Name four surface finishes for metal.
14) Explain the difference between thermoplastics and thermosetting plastics. Name two examples of each.
15) What is Tufnol made of?
16) Explain what 'shape memory alloys' are.
17) How is clay hardened in the manufacture of ceramics?
18) Name two uses of ceramics other than pottery and tableware.
19) Explain the difference between animal, vegetable, regenerated and synthetic fibres. Give an example of each.
20) Give examples of the uses and properties of nylon, lycra, cotton and wool.
21) Name five different groups of food. Name a source of each.
22) Give four useful characteristics of eggs.
23) What are the three parts of a system?
24) Draw the circuit symbols for the following electrical components: switch, light-dependent resistor, buzzer, motor, battery, LED.
25) Name four types of motion used in mechanical systems.
26) What is 'mechanical advantage'?
27) Draw sketches of the following mechanisms: cams, linkages and gears.

Hand Tools

It's not all fancy high-tech stuff in this section. You need to know about hand tools too.

Saws are the Main Cutting Tools

1) Different saws have teeth designed for cutting different materials. Tenon saws and crosscut saws are used on wood. Hacksaws are used for cutting metals and plastics. Coping saws can be used on either wood or plastic, and are mainly for cutting curves.
2) Saws have to be kept sharp, either by sharpening (e.g. tenon saw) or replacing the blade (e.g. coping saw).

Crosscut saw
Wood

Tenon saw
Wood

Hacksaw
Metal and plastic

Coping saw
Wood and plastic

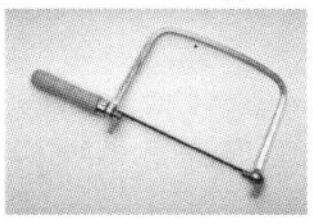

Planes and Files are Used for Shaping and Smoothing

1) This is a bench plane:

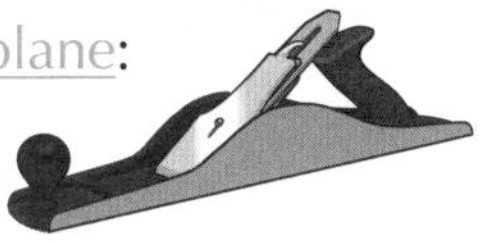

2) It has an angled blade that shaves off thin layers of material.
3) It's used on wood for removing material (shaping).

1) Files have hundreds of small teeth to cut away at a material.
2) Different cuts of file make them suitable for different processes: rough cuts are for removal of material, fine cuts are for finishing (final smoothing).
3) Most files are meant for metals and plastics, but there are special ones with very coarse teeth called cabinet rasps (or rasp files) for use on wood.

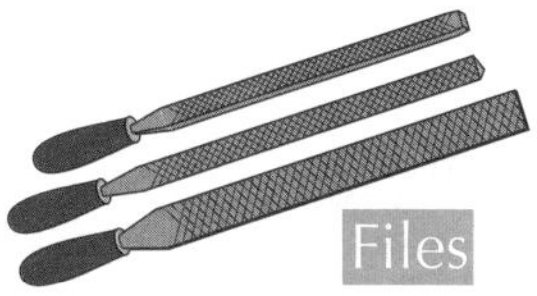

Files

Drills Make Holes (no kidding...)

Hand drill

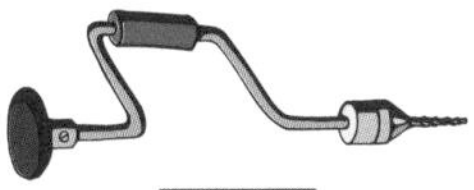

Brace

Bradawl

Twist bit

Flat bit

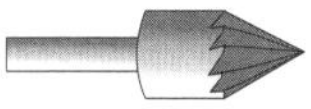

Countersink bit

1) Hand drills, braces and bradawls are hand tools for making holes. There are also machine drills and hand-held power drills. All drills rotate the drill bit clockwise and press it against the material.
2) Twist bits are used for drilling small holes into wood, metals and plastics.
3) Flat bits are used on wood and plastics to drill large flat-bottomed holes.
4) Countersink bits make holes for screw heads to sit in.
5) Different bits are suitable for different materials. Auger bits are used on wood. High speed steel (HSS) twist bits are used on metals and plastics.

Chisels are Used for Shaping Woods and Metals

1) Wood chisels (bevel-edged, firmer and mortise chisels) are used on wood and are hit with a mallet.
2) Cold chisels are used on metals and are hit with a hammer.
3) Gouges are chisels with a curved cutting edge — they're used for sculpting.

Wood chisels

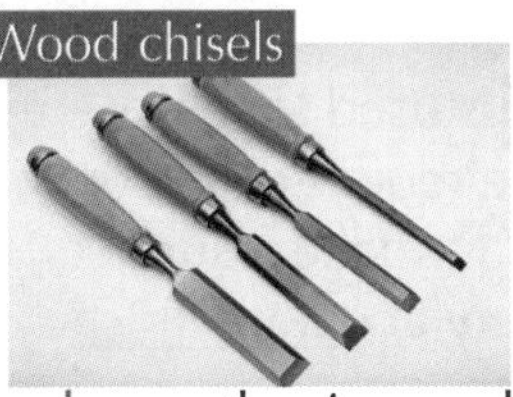

Cold chisel

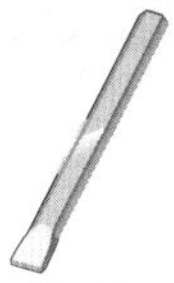

Gouges

Learn about tools — you know the drill...

Before removing material always mark out what's to be removed and then double-check your marking out. It's a bit tricky to stick stuff back on if you've cut it off by mistake.

Machine Tools

Machines tools do the same jobs as manual tools — but a lot quicker and more accurately.

Machine Tools are Quick and Accurate

1) These are usually stationary and are often bolted to the workbench or the floor.
2) They can be used for processing large quantities of material accurately and quickly.
3) Most machines used for wood are attached to a dust extractor.
4) Safety glasses should be used and clothing tucked in to avoid catching in machines.

There are some Ace Machines for Cutting and Drilling

The circular saw or saw bench has a round blade and is used to cut wood and man-made wooden materials like plywood to size. It makes straight cuts only.

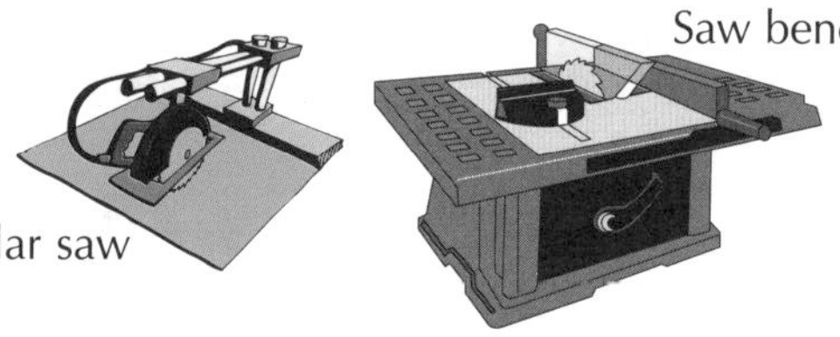

Saw bench

Circular saw

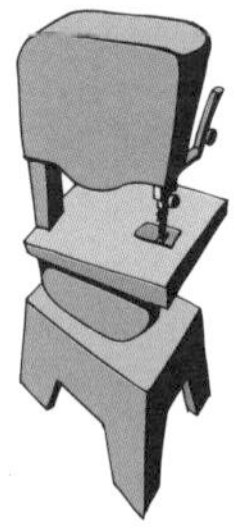

The band saw has a blade in a long flexible loop and is normally used to cut wood, but special blades can be bought for use on plastics and softer metals. The blades come in different widths and can be used for straight or curved cuts.

A planer and thicknesser (either separate or both in a single machine) are used for flattening the surface of pieces of wood and for reducing their thickness to a specified measurement.

A pillar drill or pedestal drill is used with HSS twist bits, or other types of suitable bit, to make round holes.
They can be used on all kinds of materials, depending on the bit used.

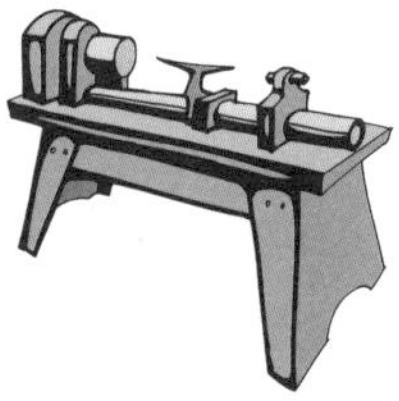

Lathes come in two types — wood lathes and engineers' lathes (for working metal). A piece of material is held and rotated by the lathe, while the turning tool or cutting bit is pressed onto the material to cut it. Lathes are mostly used to produce cylindrical objects.

A bench grinder contains abrasive wheels of different grades (coarse to smooth).
It's used to remove metal for shaping or finishing purposes, as well as for sharpening edged tools such as chisels.

A milling machine is used to remove metal one thin layer at a time to produce the required size or shape.
It can also be used to make a surface absolutely flat.
It can produce a very accurate finish.

All this information is giving me a saw head...

Machines are cool, don't you reckon — especially compared with doing it by hand. Personally, I'm hopeless at sawing — never get it in a straight line and generally cut myself. Not fun. But give me a saw bench and I'm your... um... person. Lovely neat edges and no missing fingers. Smashing.

Jigs, Moulds and Templates

Jigs, moulds and templates are pretty handy things all round — they save you a lot of work. In industry they're used to increase the speed and efficiency of the production process.

Templates are Used to Make Repetitive Shapes

1) Templates are very easy to make and simple to use.
2) You can use them to reproduce any number of identical shapes from one original pattern (template). The original is used to draw, scribe or cut round.
3) Templates need to be strong and hard-wearing so that they can be used repetitively without wearing down.
4) Afterwards, the components can be checked against the templates for accuracy.

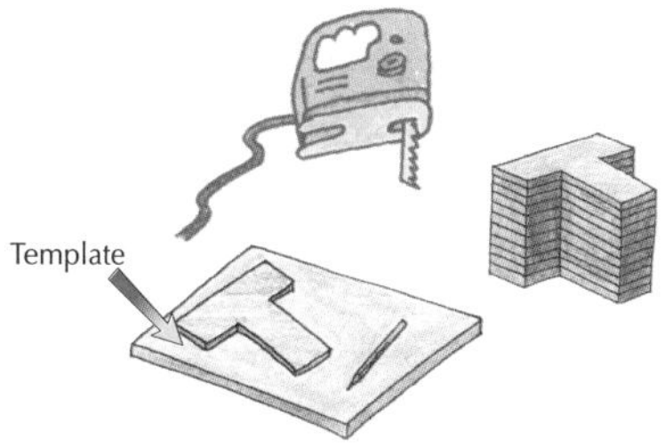

Jigs Help Manufacture Repetitive Components

1) A jig guides the tools that are working on a component.
2) Jigs come in many different shapes and sizes and can be specifically made for a particular job.
3) They're designed to speed up production and simplify the making process.
4) A drilling jig gets rid of the need for complex marking out. It can also help cut down on errors, and make sure every component is identical.
5) Some jigs are a standard size and shape and could be used on many different jobs. E.g. a dovetail jig enables complex dovetail joints (see p57) to be machined with a router, very quickly and easily, and with minimal measuring and marking out.

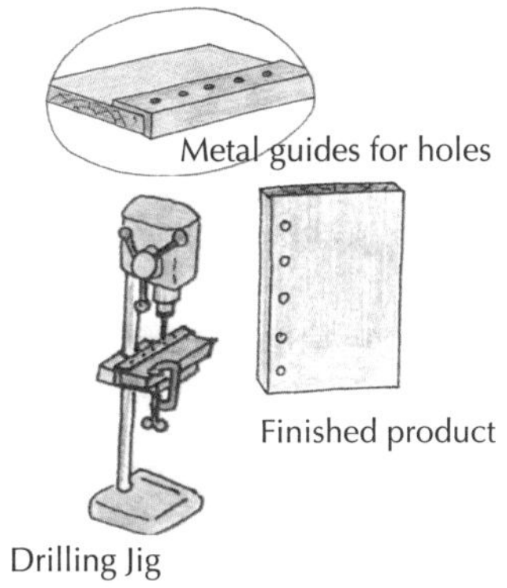

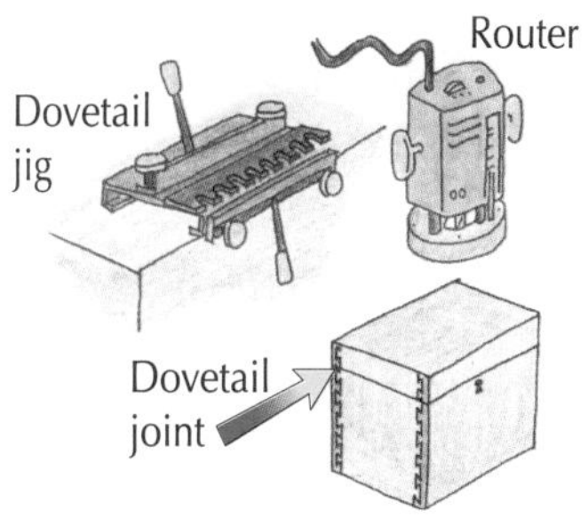

Moulds — Reproduce 3D Shapes

1) Moulds are most commonly used in plastics manufacturing, in processes such as vacuum forming, compression moulding and blow moulding. See p53-54 for more on moulding.
2) Once an accurate mould has been made, detailed plastic shapes can be formed with it over and over again.
3) Industrial moulds are expensive to produce, so a manufacturer needs to be certain of their design, and needs to be able to make large numbers of their product to make it cost-effective.

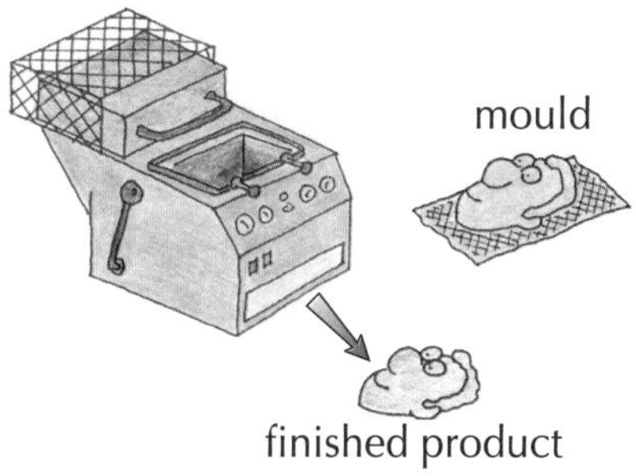

Design Your Own Jigs, Moulds and Templates...

In lessons, you could design and make very simple jigs, moulds or templates to help you produce some of your components. By doing this you will also be able to illustrate how, in theory, you could put your product into small-scale batch production.

No — this page has nothing to do with Scottish dancing...

This is a pretty groovy section. It's got all those colourful little pictures and everything. Learn how this stuff saves time in industry and how it could be used to improve *your* project.

Deforming

Deforming means changing the shape of a material.

Laminating is Gluing Thin Strips of Wood Together

1) Thin strips of wood (usually 2-6 mm thick) are glued together, like plywood.
2) This 'sandwich' is held in a jig, which keeps it in the shape of the finished product whilst the glue dries.
3) Items produced this way include chair and table legs, roof beams and rocking chair runners.

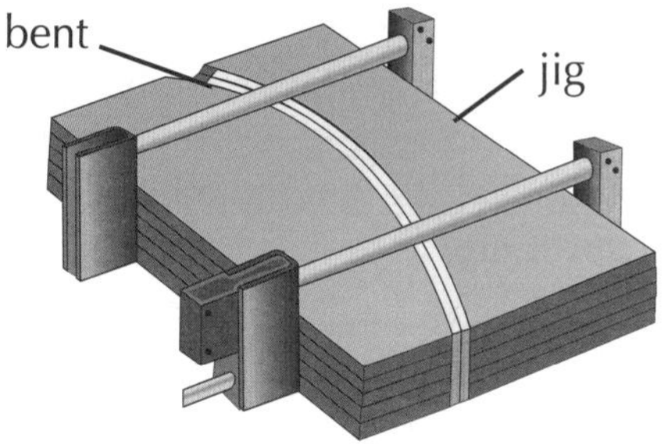

Most Metals need to be Heated before Bending

1) Some thin pieces of metal can be bent cold on a jig or former.
2) Thicker or harder (ferrous) metals have to be brought to red heat in order to bend them. Non-ferrous metals have to be taken to annealing temperature first, and allowed to cool before bending.
3) This makes them soft enough to bend easily, but the annealing process might have to be repeated as bending makes them go hard again ('work hardening').

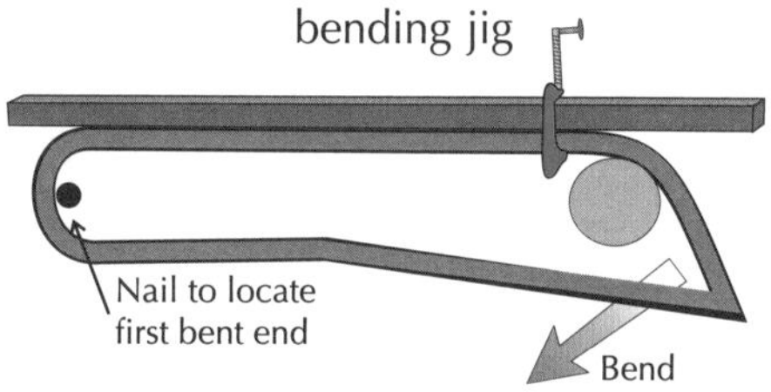

Sheet Metals can be Folded...

1) This is a method of shaping sheet metals such as aluminium and tin plate.
2) The outline of the product, e.g. a box, is marked out and cut from a flat sheet of metal.
3) The sides are then bent or folded up using folding bars, formers and mallets.
4) The corners are then joined using rivets, soldering, brazing, etc.

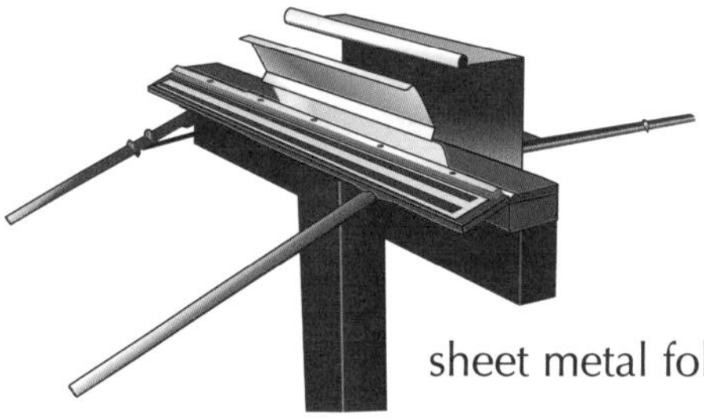

...and so can Plastics...

1) Line bending is ideal for use with acrylic sheets — e.g. for making picture frames and pencil holders, etc.
2) With the bend-line softened on a strip heater the required bend can be made by hand or using a suitable jig.

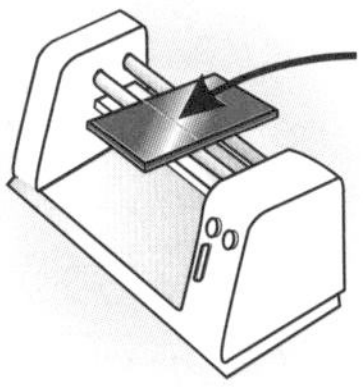

The element heats the plastic along the line where you want to bend it.

Iron and Steel are Forged

1) Metal, especially iron and steel, can be heated in a forge. A forge is a fire with air blown into the middle of it to produce a very hot flame.
2) When the metal's hot enough to have softened sufficiently, it's taken out and hammered into shape on an anvil.

Dave said he'd deform my nose if I kept seeing his girlfriend...

If you're making something out of metal, you might find that you end up using iron or steel. Now, iron and steel can be forged. But if I were you, I'd use the real stuff. It's probably better.

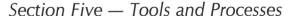

Deforming

Most of these processes involve heat — so take necessary safety precautions.

Press Moulding is Used to Shape Thermosets

1) A 'slug' of thermosetting plastic powder is put into a 'female' mould.
2) A former is pressed onto it and pushes the plastic into the mould.
3) Very high temperatures and pressures liquify the powder, and the plastic is set into a permanent shape.

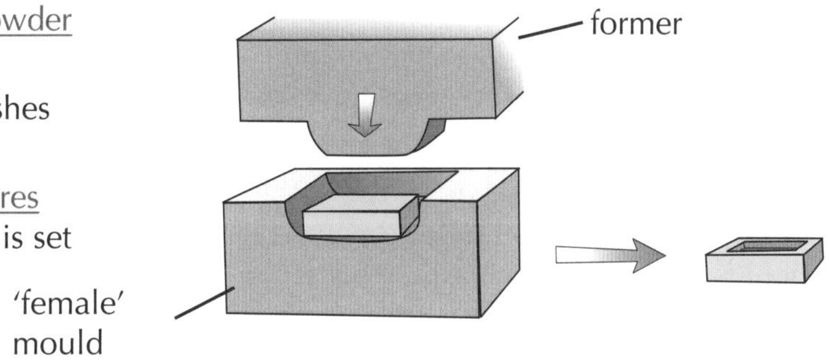

In Vacuum Forming, Air is Sucked from Round the Mould

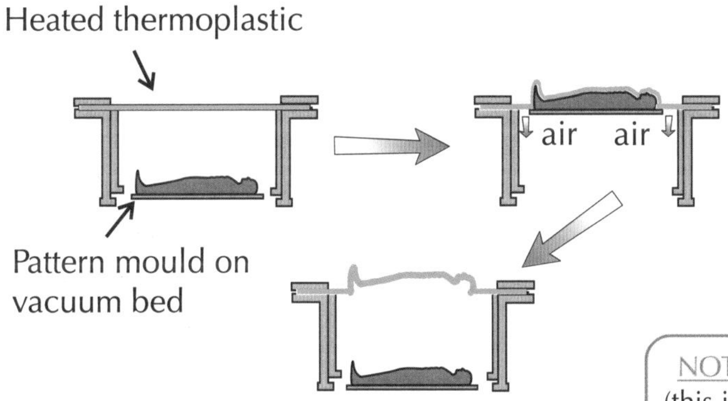

1) A sheet of thermoplastic is heated until it goes soft.
2) A pattern (or male mould) is put onto the vacuum bed. The bed is then lifted close to the heated plastic.
3) The air is sucked out from under the plastic. Atmospheric pressure forces the plastic onto the pattern mould.

NOTE: The sides of the pattern must be slightly tapered (this is called the draught angle) and the corners rounded to allow the finished product to release from the mould.

Blow Moulding Uses Air

1) A sheet of thermoplastic is clamped to the bed of the former and is heated until soft.
2) Air is blown under it, which forces the plastic up through a large hole in the bed.
3) This forms a bubble or dome, and is used to make dome-shaped products.

thermoplastic bowl

A more versatile method is where the softened plastic sheet is blown into a solid mould:

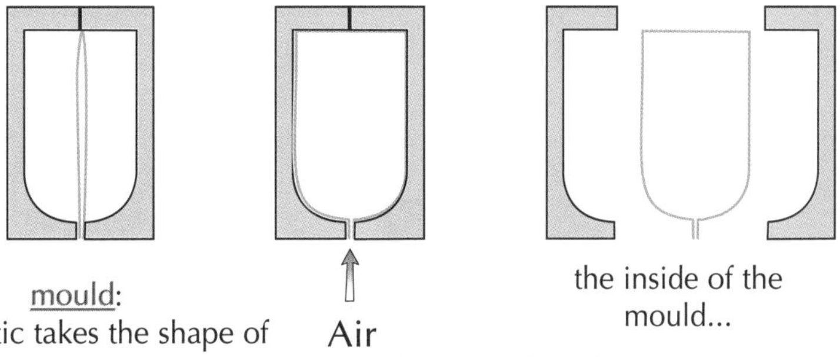

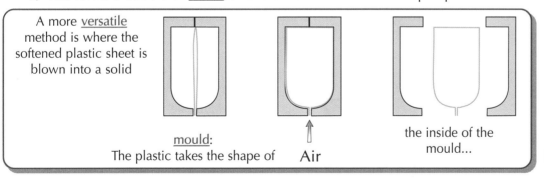

The plastic takes the shape of the inside of the mould...

...which is then opened to remove the product.
This method is often used to produce bottles and containers.

Pop Idol moulding is used to make Darius, Gareth, Will...yuk...

It's not that hard to remember this stuff — press moulding uses pressure, vacuum forming works by creating a vacuum and blow moulding works by blowing air into the plastic. Once you've got that, you need to learn the diagram for each, and an example of what you could make that way.

Reforming

Reforming is where metals or plastics are liquified, usually by heat and pressure, and then shaped in some form of mould. How absolutely amazing. This stuff really keeps me on the edge of my seat.

Die Casting is Used to Mould Metals and Thermoplastics

1) Die casting is a process used to mould metals and thermoplastics.
2) The material is melted and poured into a mould which is in the shape of the product.
3) Some plastic resins can be cold-poured into moulds (without heating). They harden or set through a chemical reaction.

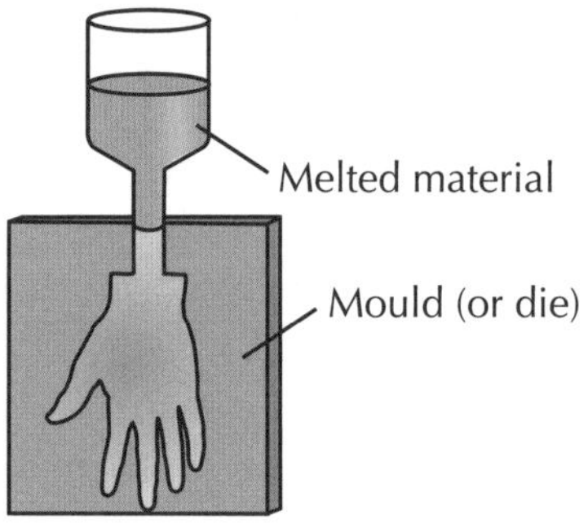

Injection Moulding Uses Pressure to Mould Plastics

1) This is similar to casting, but the molten material is forced into a closed mould under pressure.
2) The plastic is often melted using built-in heaters.
3) This is an industrial process which is usually automatic and continuous.

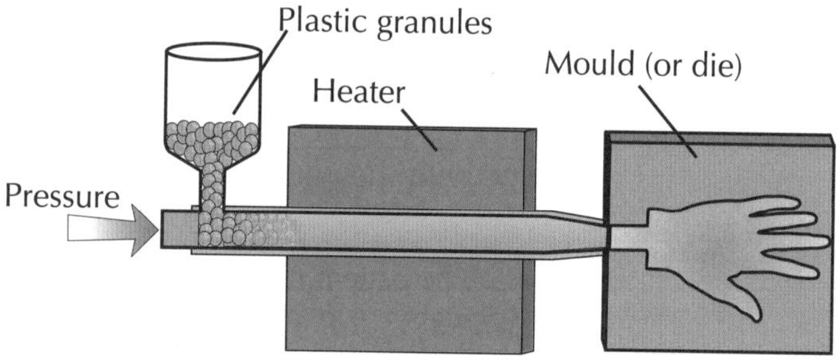

This is how you can make yourself that pink plastic hand you always wanted.

Plastics expert Brian had doubts about his new job.

Extrusion Produces Long, Continuous Strips

1) Used for some metals and thermoplastics, this process is very similar to injection moulding.
2) The material is melted and forced under pressure through a die.
3) It produces long, continuous strips of the moulding, conforming exactly to the shape of the exit hole, such as plastic-covered wire, and plastic and aluminium edgings.

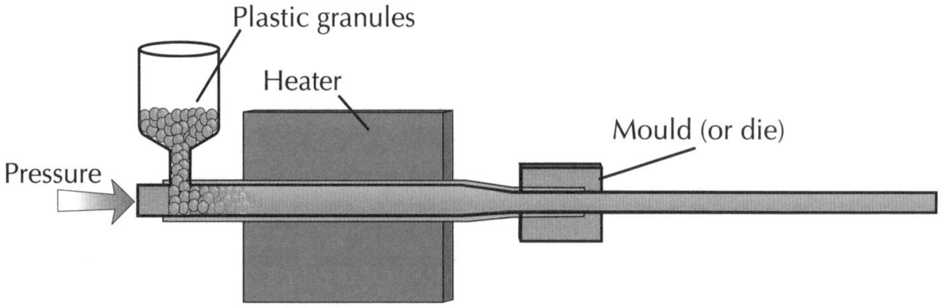

Don't eat this book — because this page is all mould-y...

Reforming processes are usually industrial processes for mass production, and are not usually economically viable for small quantities of products. Like my life-size model of Eamonn Holmes.

Fabricating — Screws and Bolts

Fabricating is the joining of pieces using the most appropriate method.
Different methods are used for different materials and in different situations.

Screws and Bolts are Used with Woods, Metals and Plastics

1) There are different types of screws for use with wood, metals, and plastics.
2) Woodscrews often require 'pilot' and 'clearance' holes to be drilled before the screw is inserted. As the screw is turned by a screwdriver, the thread (the twisty bit around the outside of the screw) pulls it into the wood. Different types of head are available for different jobs, e.g. round, countersunk, slotted and cross heads.

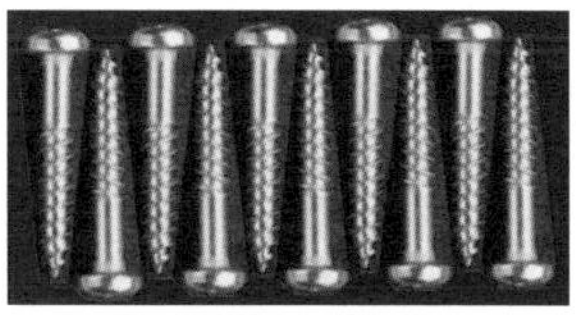

Woodscrews

3) Self-tapping screws have hardened threads that cut their own threaded holes in hard materials such as (thin) metals and hard plastics. Even with hardened threads, self-tapping screws should enter pilot holes the same size as their core diameter.
4) Machine screws have a straight shank and are used with washers and nuts. Heads vary (round, pan, countersunk, etc.). Some are tightened with a screwdriver (cross and slotted types), and some with an Allen key (socket head).

Self-tapping screws

5) Bolts are similar to machine screws but have a square or hexagonal head and are tightened with spanners.
6) Screws and bolts are usually made from steel, brass or stainless steel, and are 'self-finished' or plated with zinc, brass, chrome, or black japan (a black varnish).

Threading is Often Used to Make Joints More Secure

1) Threading is a method of fastening machine screws and bolts directly into a metal or plastic component without using nuts.
2) A hole is drilled and a set of 'taps' used to cut a female thread in the hole. The screw is inserted into it and tightened until it stops.
3) A round rod can be made to fit a threaded hole by cutting a male thread onto the outside of the rod. Male threads are cut either with a 'split die' or on a lathe. This allows components to be joined directly without the use of bolts or screws.

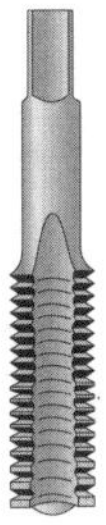

Tap

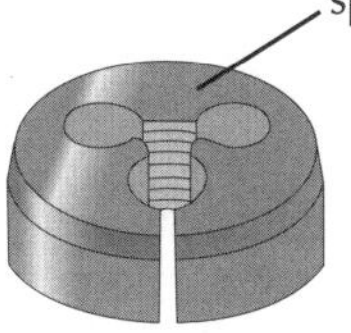

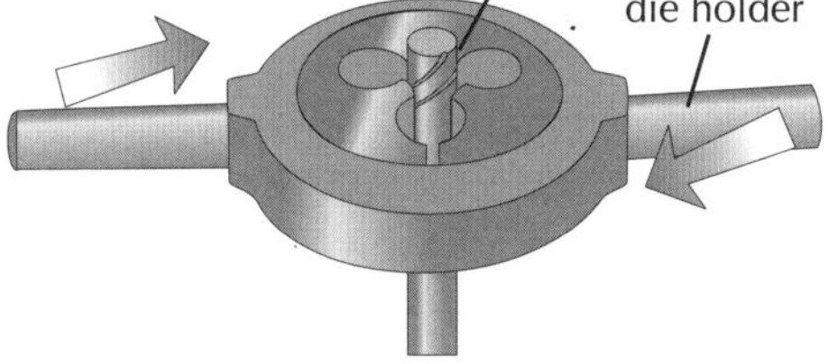

If you don't learn this page you'll be scr... um... scuppered...

Remember, screws are much like people in some ways — they have different shaped heads. But in other ways they're very different — for example, I've never seen anyone with a countersunk head.

Fabricating — Nails, Rivets and Adhesives

Nails and rivets and threads — the fun never stops with Product Design. Ah, no, I tell a lie — the fun always stops with Product Design. Much better — that first one didn't sound right at all.

Nails are Used for Joining Bits of Wood Together

1) These are similar in use to woodscrews but have a straight shank with no thread.
2) They're inserted with a hammer and can be punched below the surface with a nail punch to hide the head.
3) Nails are only used in wood and wooden products, e.g. plywood. They're much quicker to use than screws, but the joint they make is nowhere near as strong.
4) Nails are mostly made from steel, but special ones can be made from other metals, e.g. brass for use in boat building. Like screws, they come with a variety of head and shank shapes for different uses.

Panel pin

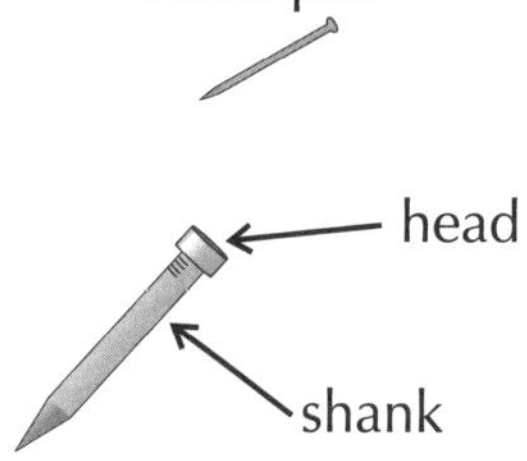

Round wire nail

Rivets are Mainly Used for Joining Sheet Metal

1) A rivet is a metal peg with a head on one end, used for joining sheet metal.
2) A hole is drilled through both pieces of metal and the rivet is inserted with a 'set' (hammer-like tool). The head is held against the metal whilst the other end is flattened and shaped into another head with a hammer.

Standard rivets

3) 'Pop' (or 'blind') rivets are now very common. They can be used where there is only access to one side of the material (hence 'blind' rivet). It's a fast and easy method of joining sheet metal.

> 1) Both rivet and pin are placed in the hole in the material.
> 2) The pin is pulled tight with a riveter (or pop gun) until it snaps off.
> 3) Pulling the pin tight causes the end of the rivet to expand and form a head on the other side.

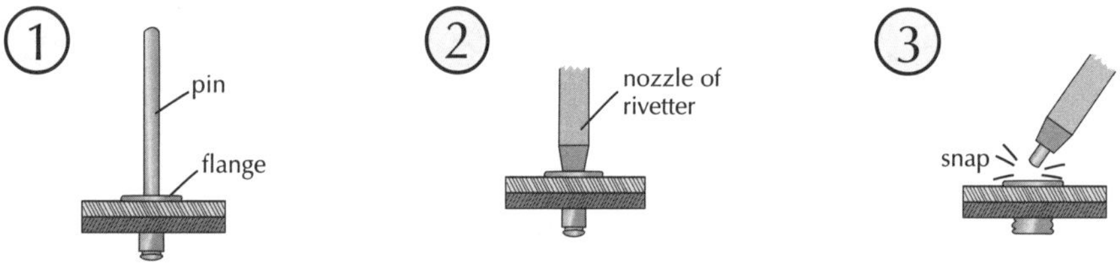

You Need to Choose the Right Adhesive for the Job

1) There are many different types of adhesive for use with different materials and for different jobs, e.g. PVA and animal glue (for wood), contact adhesive and epoxy resin (for lots of materials).
2) Adhesives will only work properly if the right one is chosen for the job, and if the surfaces to be joined are thoroughly cleaned.
3) Some plastics can't be glued as they're too smooth, and have a greasy texture which stops the glue from 'keying in'.
4) Adhesives are often used to reinforce other methods of fabrication, e.g. joints in wood.

You often get a little tube of PVA wood glue with flat-pack furniture to reinforce joints.

That page was riveting...

When deciding which method of fabrication to use on a product, think carefully about which is more important — speed of assembly or strength. It's often a trade-off between the two.

Fabricating — Joints

Wood can be joined together in several ways — either by the traditional method of cutting joints and nailing and gluing together, or by using special fittings which can be taken apart again.

Some Joints are More Permanent than Others

1) There are dozens of different joints, e.g. dovetail, mortise & tenon, housing, halving and mitred, for use in different situations. It's important to use the right joint in the right place.
2) Joints are often glued to make them secure and permanent.
3) Marking out and cutting joints takes a lot of skill.
Accuracy is vital if the joint is to fit and hold together (as well as look good).

BUTT JOINT

Pretty feeble but very quick and simple. Often used for joints in cheap pine furniture.

MITRED JOINT

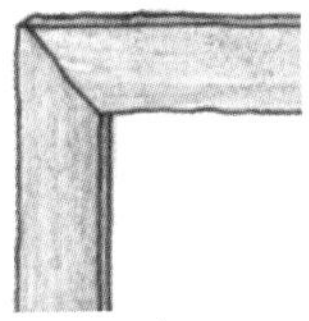

Mitred joints are similar to butt joints but prettier and trickier to cut. Used for picture frames.

DOWEL JOINT

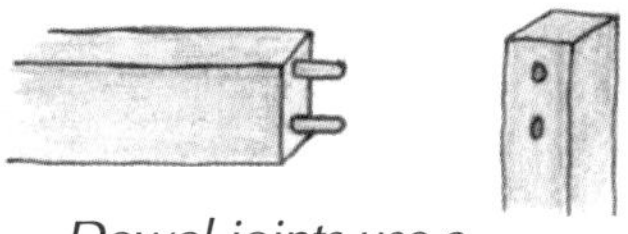

Dowel joints use a wooden or plastic peg, called a dowel, which fits into aligned holes to reinforce the joint. Often replace traditional joints in factory-made furniture.

MORTISE AND TENON

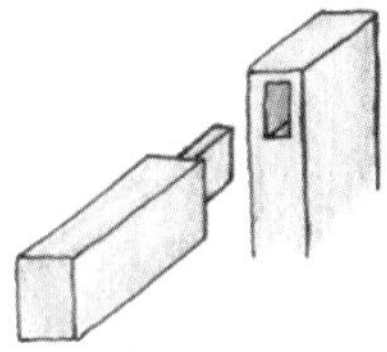

Mortise and tenon joints (cut with a tenon saw and mortise chisel) are dead strong. Often used in tables and chairs.

LAP JOINT

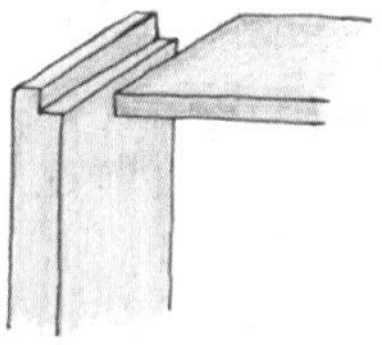

Lap joints have a larger surface area for gluing than butt joints, so they're a bit stronger. Used in some drawers and boxes.

HALVING JOINT

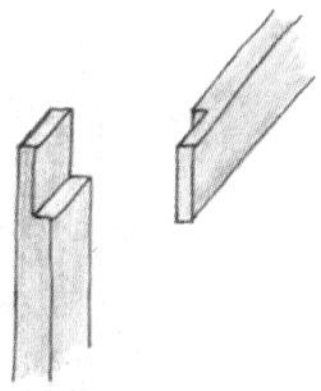

Halving joints are fairly strong — again, due to the large surface area for gluing. Sometimes used in frame construction.

HOUSING JOINT

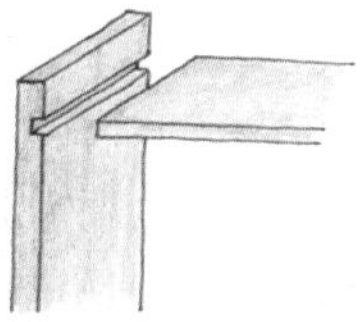

Housing joints are often used in shelving units as they provide a good surface area for gluing, and the shelf is supported all the way along its width.

DOVETAIL JOINT

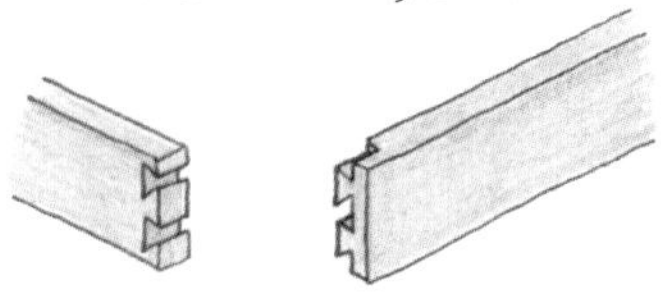

Dovetail joints are very strong and look attractive. They're often used in drawer construction. They're the bee's knees, but they're a pain in the neck to make. Unless you have a dovetail jig (see p51).

Knock-Down Fittings are Non-Permanent Joints

1) These are blocks, brackets (plastic or metal) and other fittings which enable furniture to be assembled and taken apart again easily.
2) They are used instead of traditional joints, and are very fast to use, but are nowhere near as strong as glued joints.
3) Most types are assembled with screwdrivers or Allen keys.
4) They are usually used for cheap 'flat-pack' furniture.

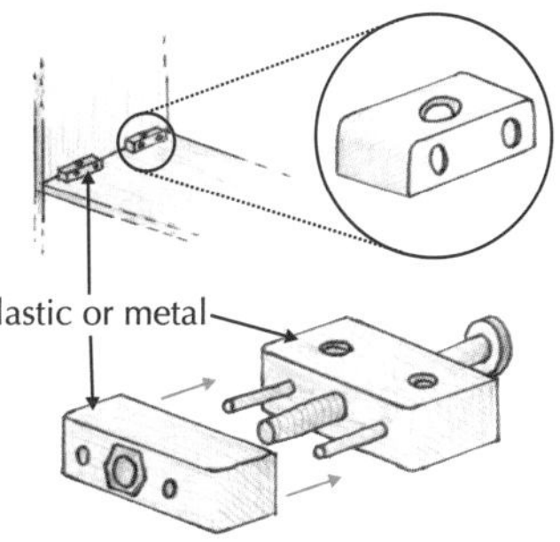

Butt joints — joined at the hip...

So, just to wrap up... which joint you use depends on:
a) whether you're a traditionalist, b) how much time you've got, c) how good you are at woodwork, d) whether you want to take the thing apart again, e) how strong you want the joint to be.

Fabricating — Joining Metals

It's the page you've been waiting for — it's all about welding and stuff. Splendid.

Soldering, Brazing & Welding are for Joining Metal

These are methods of joining metal by the use of varying amounts of heat.

1) Soldering is a relatively low temperature process. Solder, made from tin and lead, is melted onto the components to be joined, bonding them together when it cools and solidifies. A soldering iron or blow torch can be used for this process.

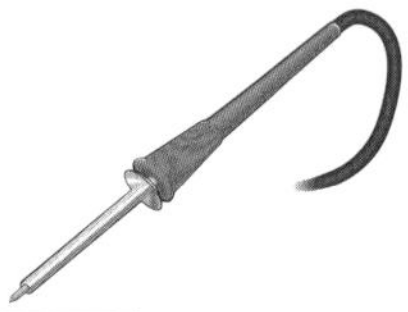

Soldering Iron

2) Brazing is a higher temperature process which uses brass spelter as the joining material. Either a gas brazing torch, a blow torch, or a brazing attachment for an electric-arc welder is used to heat the joint.

Blow torch

3) Welding uses a very high temperature from an oxyacetylene torch, an electric-arc welder or a TIG welder to actually melt the edges of the joint so that they flow together. Thinned metal or slight gaps are filled with metal from a welding rod. This is by far the strongest method of joining metal.

Welding equipment — the mask protects your face, particularly your eyes, from heat and sparks.

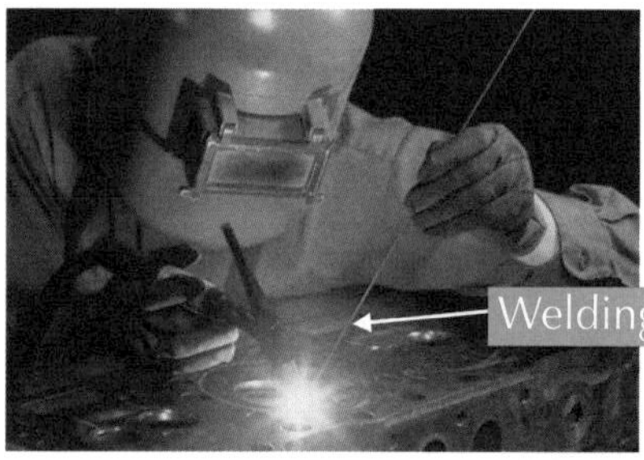

Welding rod

The Joint Needs to be Carefully Prepared

For all three of the above processes careful preparation of the joint is vital:

1) Joints have to be well-fitting with minimal gaps.
2) They must also be very clean and free from grease. Fingerprints on the surface can stop solder or brass spelter from 'taking'.
3) 'Flux' has to be used when soldering and brazing and on some metals when welding. This stops the air oxidising the surface of the metal whilst heating it, as this too would stop the joint from taking.

Doughnuts — for while you work

Marty has to get to 88 mph to make the flux capacitor work...

Extra care needs to be taken with heat processes. And make sure you use the safety and protective clothing and equipment provided. And don't try and solder your hand to your face. It'll hurt.

Fixtures and Fittings

There are many fixtures and fittings available on the market.
You can use these for locking, hinging and joining. Sounds like fun.

There Are Four Main Types of Hinge

Hinges are available in steel, brass and nylon, and can be coated to match a piece of furniture.
The part of the hinge that moves is called the knuckle.

1) Butt hinges are the most common type of hinge used for hanging doors.
2) The two parts of the hinge are set into the door and frame.
3) They're available in brass or steel.

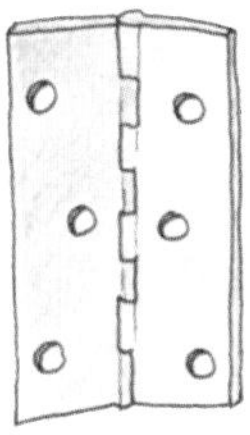

1) Flush hinges are screwed directly onto the surface of the wood, so they're easier to fit than butt hinges.
2) They're usually used for lightweight jobs.

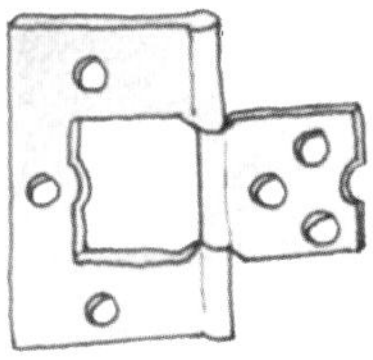

1) Tee hinges are often used outside — for things like shed doors or garden gates. The longer 'strap' allows the hinge to support a greater weight.
2) They're often covered in black enamel.

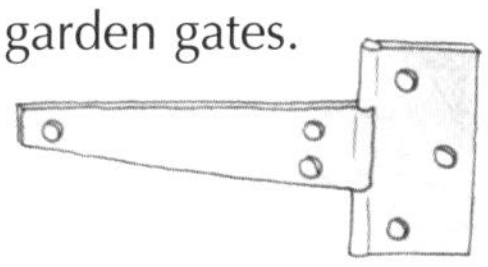

1) Pivot hinges are used when you might need to lift a door off its frame.
2) One part of the hinge is screwed to the door and the other to the door frame.

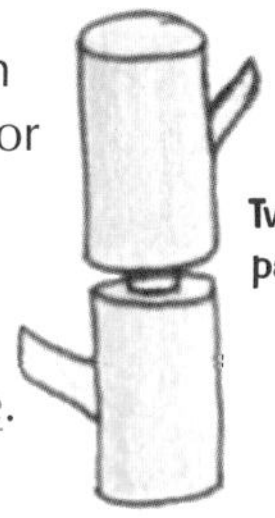

Two separate parts that fit together.

Most Locks and Catches Are Made from Steel or Brass

Locks need to be strong, and so tend to be made from steel, plated steel or brass.

1) Cupboard locks are screwed to the edge of cupboard doors.
2) No cutting is required when fitting the lock.
3) They can be used for both left and right locking.

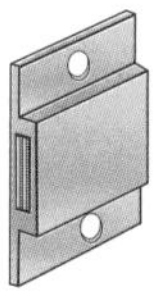

magnetic catch

1) Catches hold a door closed without locking.
2) They can be made out of brass, steel and various plastics.

spring catch

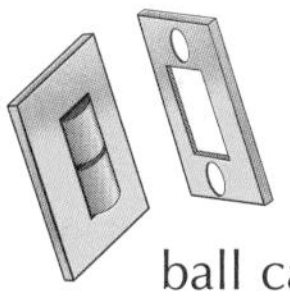

ball catch

Other Fixtures & Fittings

1) Shelving fitments allow a shelf to be placed into position.
2) They do not require cutting into the shelf.
3) The fitments are able to be repositioned for different shelf heights.

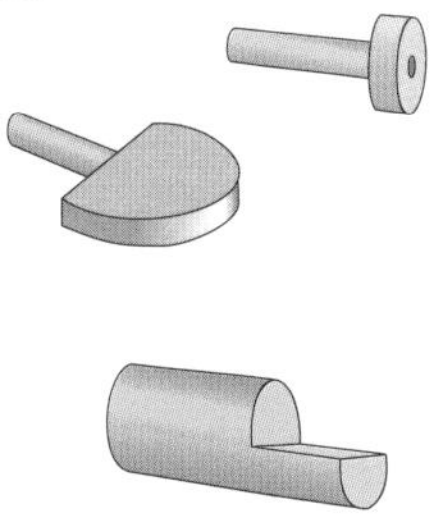

1) Leg fastenings can be used to attach legs to tables or chairs where the joints need to be frequently taken apart.
2) They also offer reinforcement, making the joint stronger.

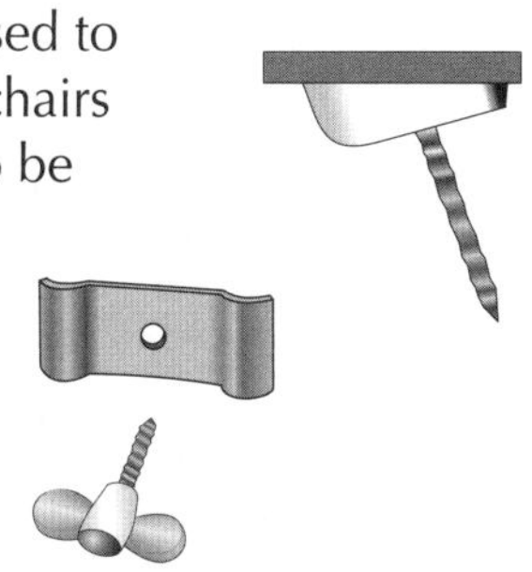

Your grade could HINGE on how well you know this...

hahaha hahahaha ha... ha... um...

Fixtures and fittings... I mean, wow... I bet you thought the page was going to be a bit boring. You didn't think it was going to be as racy as this. You probably need to get your breath back after that page. Well, go and have a cup of tea, and come back to this in five minutes. You deserve it.

Fillers and Finishing

Finishes are things like paint which are applied to a product to protect it from damage and make it look good. Before you apply a finish, most surfaces will need some kind of preparation...

Fillers Prepare Surfaces for Finishing

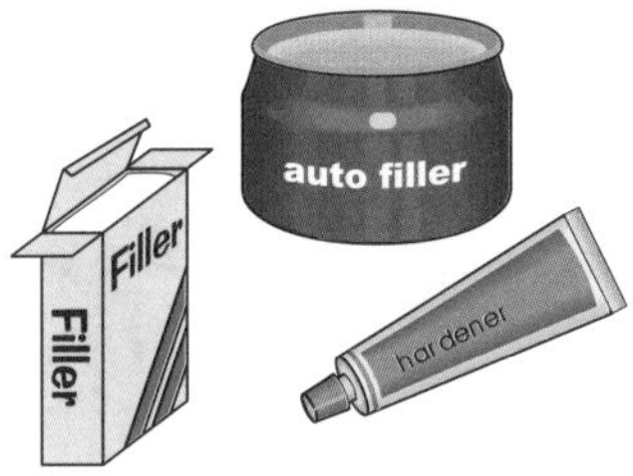

1) Car-body filler (David's Isopon) is a two-part resin-based product, which, when mixed, sets to a tough finish that can then be machined (i.e. drilled, filed, etc.).
2) Polyfilla is powder that's mixed with water to make a thick paste. This can fill small cracks and improve the surface finish on rough wood and foam models. It sets quickly and can be smoothed with glass paper.
3) Plaster of Paris is a fine white powder, which, when mixed with water, soon sets to a very hard finish. It's used with bandages to set broken limbs and to produce landscape features on scale models. It can be cast in a mould.
4) Art Roc or Modroc is a bandage material impregnated with plaster of Paris. It's great for creating textured landscape surfaces too, particularly when painted.

Laminating and Varnishing Make Work Look Smart

1) Laminating (or encapsulation) is a quick and effective way to finish a piece of work on paper or thin card. Laminating uses heat to sandwich the paper or card between two layers of plastic. This gives a professional finish to posters, menus, bookmarks, etc.
2) Spirit varnish/lacquers consist of a synthetic (man-made) resin (e.g. acrylic resin, cellulose resin) dissolved in an organic solvent. The solvent evaporates to leave a thin protective layer of varnish. Varnish/lacquer can be applied with a brush or spray can.

Paints are made from Pigment dissolved in a 'Vehicle'

1) Paints are made up of a pigment (a colour) and a 'vehicle' (a solvent — something that carries the pigment).
2) There's a whole load of different 'vehicles', like water, acrylic, cellulose, oil, etc.
3) Once the paint has been applied, the vehicle evaporates to leave just the pigment.
4) Pigments may be made from chemicals, rocks or plants. Woad, which used to be used to dye jeans blue, comes from a plant.
5) Paints can be brushed on, or sprayed on from a can.
6) Before paint is applied you must remove visible marks with files, emory cloth, glasspaper etc and then remove any grease or dust.

Several thin coats of paint, stain, varnish, etc. look better than one thick coat.

I wanted to finish with my girlfriend, so I laminated her...

(Oh come on, you didn't believe me did you...)

Learn which fillers and finishes are best for which surfaces. You wouldn't want to spoil a model you'd spent ages on by messing up the finish, would you? Oh no, no, no, no.

Packaging and Waste

Packaging protects, preserves and promotes the product it contains — they're called "the 3 Ps" by people in the packaging industry... maybe.

Protection — during Transit and from Customers

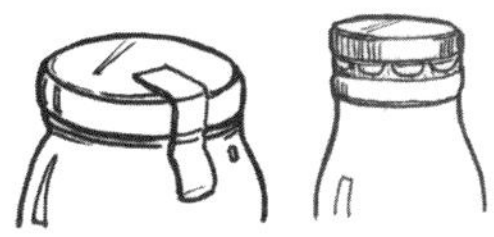

1) Packaging materials like cardboard and expanded polystyrene can protect a product from knocks and bumps during transportation.
2) Manufacturers can also add tamper-evident seals to packaging to try and prevent customers tampering with products.

Preservation — especially Foodstuffs

1) Many products (especially foodstuffs) begin to deteriorate when exposed to oxygen in the air.
2) Sealed glass jars and bottles, 'tin' cans and tubes are traditional packages for foodstuffs, drinks and toothpaste.
3) However, plastics and composite materials (e.g. layers of card, plastic and aluminium foil laminated together) are being used more and more these days.

Promotion — to make you Buy More Stuff

1) Manufacturers often use striking colours and shapes of packaging to entice you to buy their products.
2) As well as the names of the manufacturer and the product, the packaging may include pictures or images showing how the product should be used, or a contact address (or anything else for that matter).
3) It may also include a 'flash' showing money off or a catchy slogan, e.g. '*CGP — Buy our chickens, they're ace*'.

Avoid Unnecessary Waste with the 3 Rs

Unnecessary and waste packaging is a big problem. But there are things the public and industry can do to help.

Reduction — use materials economically by using designs that tessellate (which will produce less waste). It's also a smart idea to avoid unnecessary packaging, e.g. by selling chocolates in a paper bag rather than a plastic tray in a cardboard box wrapped in cellophane.

Reusing — milk bottles, jam jars and egg boxes can be reused many times.

Recycling — recycling materials (e.g. card, glass, plastic, metal) means they can be used again to make the same or different products.

Avoid unnecessary waste — eat this book once you've read it...

I went into a shop the other day and saw a yoghurt in the fridge that had a tamper-evident seal. Anyway, I picked the yoghurt up and must have handled it a bit roughly, because the seal started barking and banging its flippers together. It gave me a right fright. And I had to buy the yoghurt.

Revision Summary

What a fantastic section. Life couldn't get better than this, not even if you discovered you were Spiderman, came up with an brilliant new invention, saved the world from nuclear extinction, made an Oscar-winning film and won a life-time's supply of bingo cards (maybe that last one's just me).
Anyway, do the questions...

1) Name four different types of hand saw. What is each one used for?
2) Name three different types of drill bit. Say what each one is used for.
3) Describe how a band saw works.
4) Name two uses of a bench grinder.
5) What are templates used for?
6) What is a jig? Why are drilling jigs useful?
7) Describe the process of laminating.
8) What is 'work hardening'?
9) What is a forge?
10) Describe the process of press moulding.
11) Draw a series of diagrams to illustrate vacuum forming.
12) How does blow moulding work, and what shape is produced in this process?
13) Explain the difference between die casting and injection moulding.
14) What shapes are produced by extrusion?
15) Name the three main types of screw. How do they differ, and what are they used for?
16) Explain the difference between a bolt and a machine screw.
17) Name the tool used to cut a female thread.
18) Describe two different ways of cutting a male thread.
19) Give one advantage and one disadvantage of using nails rather than woodscrews.
20) How does a pop rivet work?
21) Why can some plastics not be glued?
22) Name four types of wood joint.
23) What is the main disadvantage of using dovetail joints?
24) What are 'knock-down' fittings?
25) Describe the main differences between soldering, brazing and welding.
26) Why do you need to use flux when soldering and brazing? What does it do?
27) What are the four main types of hinge? Describe when each type might be used.
28) Explain the difference between a lock and a catch.
29) Name four fillers, and describe when they might be used.
30) Give two reasons why a finish might be applied to a product.
31) What is a 'vehicle', in terms of paint?
32) Describe the three purposes of packaging.
33) Explain three ways in which waste can be limited.

Scale of Production

The term 'scale of production' is all about the quantity of products that you're going to manufacture. Commercially there are four main categories for you to learn...

Jobbing Production — Making a One-Off Product

1) This is where you're making a single product.
2) Every item made will be different, to meet the customer's individual and specific requirements.
3) This type of production is very labour intensive, and requires a highly skilled workforce.
4) Examples are wide-ranging, from made-to-measure furniture to one-off buildings like the Millennium Dome.

Batch Production — A Specified Quantity of a Product

1) This is where you're making a specific quantity of a particular product.
2) Batches can be repeated as many times as required.
3) The machinery and labour used need to be flexible, so they can quickly change from making one batch to making another batch of a similar product.
4) The time between batches, when machines and tools may have to be set up differently or changed around, is called down time. This is unproductive and needs to be kept as short as possible so the manufacturer doesn't lose money.

Mass Production — High-Volume Production

1) Making products on a really large scale, such as cars or electrical goods.
2) Often uses expensive specialised equipment including computer-aided manufacturing (CAM) and industrial robots.
3) As well as all this equipment, you need a large workforce. The different stages of production and manufacture are broken down into simple repetitive tasks which people are able to learn easily.
4) Recruitment is relatively easy — you don't need to employ skilled people.

Continuous Production — Non-Stop Production 24hrs/day

1) This involves non-stop, uninterrupted production.
2) The specialised equipment required costs so much that it would be too expensive to turn it off. So it has to keep running and producing continuously.
3) Examples of continuous production include oil and chemical manufacture.

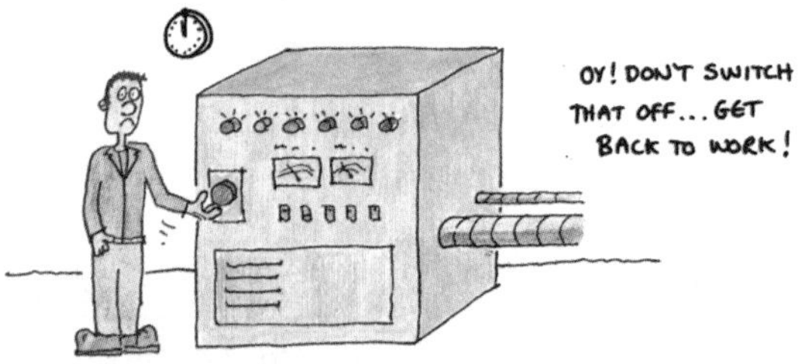

Which Category Do I Use in the School Workshop?

If you're making a single product that you've designed, with its own specification, it will be jobbing production. Sometimes you may work with the rest of the class in small teams, all making different parts of a product which you then bring together and assemble to produce a number of identical products. This will be batch production.

It's not what you've got — it's how much you've got of it...

Yup, all that this lot boils down to is quantity.

Manufacturing Systems

Commercial manufacturing can be thought of as a system made up a number of sub-systems. These sub-systems need to work together in order for the whole system to run properly.

A Manufacturing System Covers All Areas of Production

Manufacturing systems ensure the efficient and successful design and production of products. The following things need to be in place as part of the manufacturing system:

1 A Trained and Organised Workforce

- Workers should be organised into different roles in each sub-system.
- Workers should be good at communicating with everyone involved.
- They need to be trained in the skills of their specific role.

2 Specialised Buildings or Workshops

- The workplace needs to be adapted to manufacturing.
- Areas need to be designated to different uses, e.g. storage, finishing, packing.

3 Systems to help People Communicate

- Communication is very important for the smooth running of the manufacturing process.
- E-mail, telephones and fax machines all help people communicate quickly.
- Particular information might need to be communicated between departments at certain stages of production — there might be procedures in place to make sure this is done.

4 Organisation of Tools, Equipment and Materials

- The selection, ordering and storage of materials needs to be done at the right time and in the right quantities.
- Appropriate equipment is needed for the manufacturing process — it needs to be well maintained and used safely.

5 Efficient Design and Production Processes

- Design needs to be geared towards mass production e.g. use easily available materials.
- Manufacturing processes need to be able to transform raw materials and components into products.

6 Quality Control Systems

- There should be quality control checks at every stage in the manufacturing process.
- Good communication and efficient working methods should minimise the risk of mistakes.

7 Health and Safety — Risk Assessment and Safety Procedures

- Risk assessments should be carried out on the workplace, materials and processes used. Measures should be taken to minimise the risk to workers.
- Workers should follow guidelines and procedures to avoid hazards.

8 System for Disposing of Waste / Caring for the Environment

- Waste needs to be disposed of safely, with as little damage to the Environment as possible.
- If possible, recyclable or biodegrable materials should be used to minimise the environmental impact.

Page 64 — the best insomnia cure in the world ever...

There you have it — 8 things to learn that make up an efficient and successful manufacturing system.

Manufacturing Systems

Take a look at these five main manufacturing systems, and learn how they work.

Cell Production is Working in Teams to Produce Components

1) Production stages are split into individual components, which are each made by a different production cell.
2) Each cell has a team of people working to produce a single component.
3) Within each cell the team is responsible for all aspects of production, including quality control and maintenance of the machines.
4) Advantages of this method include teamwork, communication and quality.

In-Line Assembly is Used for Mass Production

1) Most of the production line is automated.
2) Unskilled labour is used mainly for assembly, with a small number of semi-skilled operators making sure there's a continuous flow along the production line.
3) A disadvantage of this system is the lack of flexibility when compared with cells.

Flexible Manufacturing Systems Use Semi-Skilled Workers

1) The FMS approach is based on the belief that the key to successful manufacturing is a flexible workforce and flexible machinery.
2) Individual people are semi-skilled, being able to do a variety of jobs.
3) It works well with batch production, where change and flexibility are essential.

Concurrent Engineering Needs Good Communication

1) This is where different stages of the design process can overlap (one can start work before the other has finished) — which saves time.
2) It's essential to make sure there are good communication links between all the stages of the design process, e.g. marketing, research, design, planning, manufacture and distribution.

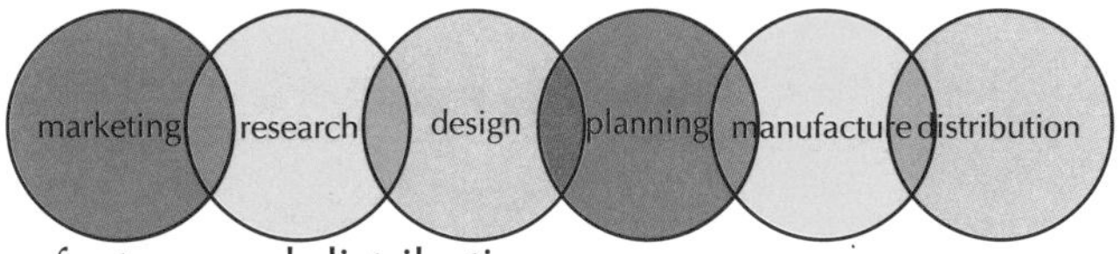

3) The overall aim is to design and make the product with maximum efficiency.

Just-in-Time Manufacturing Needs Detailed Forward Planning

1) For just-in-time manufacture (JIT), you only buy materials and components as and when you need them.
2) This removes the need for large stockpiles of resources, saving money and space.
3) Everything has to be kept on time, or things can easily go wrong.

Cell production — hold on, am I in the Biology book by mistake...

Darned useful stuff this — especially if you're going to go anywhere near the manufacturing industry when you leave school. Well, even if you're not, you still have to learn it for the old GCSEs.

Control Systems and Feedback

Systems are sets of separate things which work together to result in a task being completed.
When systems are used they are often broken down into manageable units.

Systems are Used for All Sorts...

Systems are used for things like:

- Making the process you're going to use more efficient.
- To make the task you are carrying out easier.
- Making the task and process easier to check.

A system is usually divided into three parts:

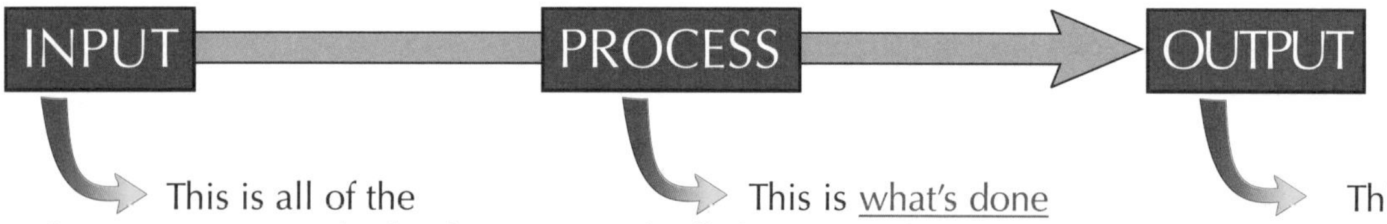

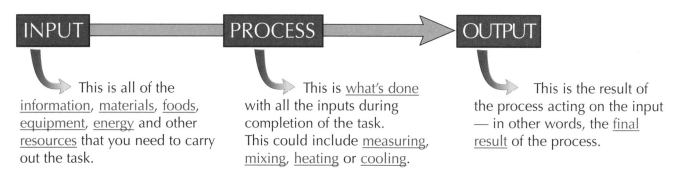

This is all of the information, materials, foods, equipment, energy and other resources that you need to carry out the task.

This is what's done with all the inputs during completion of the task. This could include measuring, mixing, heating or cooling.

This is the result of the process acting on the input — in other words, the final result of the process.

Systems Include Processes which give Feedback

Feedback may be used at each stage of production and helps to ensure good quality final products.

For example, if a pizza is being completely covered with cheese, this can be checked by a person or perhaps by a machine. If the pizza is completely covered then it can be cooked. If not, the pizza has to go back to the beginning of that stage of the process.

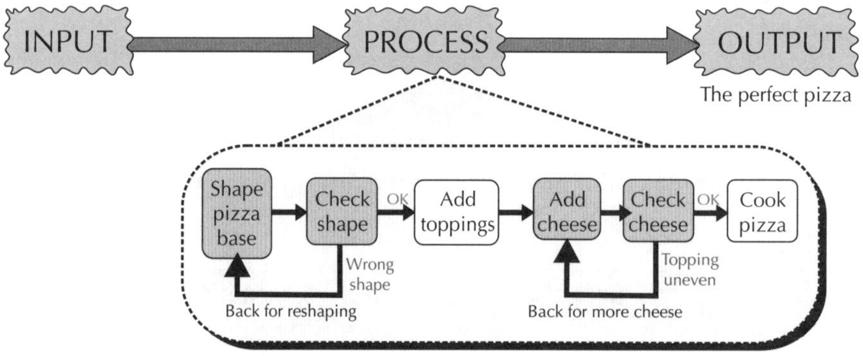

A computer may monitor a manufacturing process at each stage and give feedback.
It may then take control and return the product to a previous process stage.

This would be an example of COMPUTER-AIDED MANUFACTURE (CAM) — see page 20.

System addict — I never can give it up*...

You put a load of stuff in (INPUT), you do something to it (PROCESS) and you get something out in the end (OUTPUT) — that's a SYSTEM. In addition you can add feedback which checks the product is OK and allows problems to be fixed. Cool eh...

*This is for your teacher — get them to read it out and see if they start singing and shaking their 1980s booty.

Quality Control and Assurance

Manufacturers want customer loyalty — so they need to make sure their product is always manufactured to a high standard. These are the industry jargon words for it:

QUALITY ASSURANCE (QA) is all about standards — setting standards and meeting them.
QUALITY CONTROL (QC) is how you check whether you're meeting those standards.

Manufacturers have a System to Deal with Faults

To ensure that a product leaves the factory in good condition the manufacturer has to set up a foolproof system of checking and dealing with faults.

- Throughout the manufacturing process, products are visually checked and tested.
- Products can be checked against the detailed manufacturer's specification.
- Part of the system is feedback. If a product is not right, the information is immediately relayed back to the factory floor so the problem can be fixed quickly.

Hazard Analysis Critical Control Points (HACCP)

HACCP is a system which reduces the risk of products being damaged before they reach the consumer. All possible hazards are identified in advance and controls are put in place to prevent them happening.

Products are Tested by Quality Control

1) Quality control usually takes place at the end of a process and involves inspection, sampling and testing.
2) There is usually a Quality Control Department within the factory, which takes charge of all the testing and inspections.
3) It will also insist on putting in place whatever controls are necessary to ensure a quality product. The whole workforce will be involved in this system of controlling and checking.

Quality Control is Making Sure You're Within Tolerances

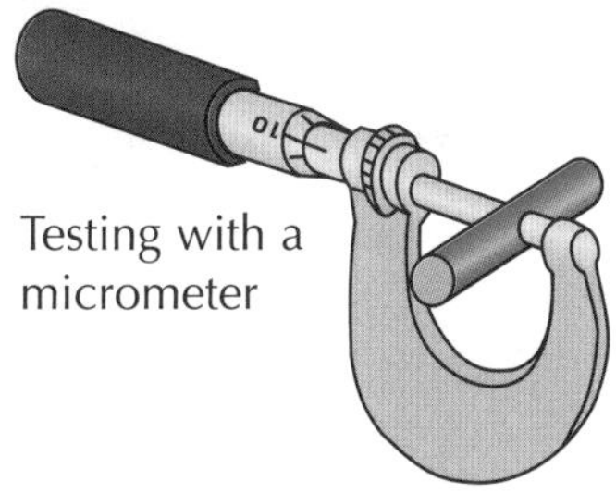

Testing with a micrometer

Quality control involves testing a sample of a component at every stage of production. It stresses the importance of working to specific tolerances — i.e. margins of error.

Tolerance in testing is expressed as an upper (+) and lower (–) deviation. For example, if a spindle is specified as being 20 mm (± 0.5), then a micrometer reading of between 19.5 mm and 20.5 mm would be OK.

Quality control makes sure a product does these things:

1) conforms to the design specification
2) does the job it was designed to do
3) meets relevant standards institutions' criteria (p29)
4) keeps the customer happy

Q: What would improve the quality of your life right now?

A: A nice holiday in Hawaii. Er... assuming that GCSE Product Design revision wasn't on offer of course... Whoo-hoo! Product Design! etc.

Revision Summary

As someone (probably called Clint) once said: "You gotta do what you gotta do" — in this case a big list of REVISION SUMMARY QUESTIONS. It's not fun. It's not easy. It doesn't taste as nice as Marmite, or run as fast as a poodle sporting go-faster stripes. But it might help you pass your exam — which is why you bought this book in the first place.

1) Give a simple definition of 'scale of production'. What are the four main types?
2) How many products would you make in jobbing production?
3) What type of production would you use to make a specific quantity of a particular product?
4) Why, in the above production method, do machinery and labour need to be flexible?
5) a) What is large-scale production (e.g. production of cars or electrical goods) called?
   b) How are the tasks broken down, and what skill level is needed of the workforce?
6) Give two examples of continuous production in industry.
7) What is the purpose of manufacturing systems?
8) Give eight things which need to be in place for a manufacturing system to run smoothly.
9) How can communication systems help a manufacturing system to run smoothly?
10) Describe cell production, and list 3 advantages of it.
11) Describe in-line assembly, and give one disadvantage of it.
12) What does FMS stand for? What does this approach see as the key to successful manufacturing?
13) What is Concurrent Engineering?
14) What does JIT stand for? What things does it eliminate?
15) Systems make manufacturing more:
    a) efficient, easy to do and easy to check
    b) efficient, easy to do and costly
    c) efficient, time-consuming and cost-effective
16) Explain what 'feedback' is in the context of systems.
17) What is quality assurance?
18) What does HACCP stand for?
19) What are tolerances?
20) If a component had to be 35 mm ± 0.2 mm, what would be the upper and lower tolerances? Would 34.7 mm be OK?

Tips on Getting Started

This section's got all the stuff people don't do that the exam boards get really annoyed about. Read this before you start your project to make sure you keep those markers happy.

Step 1 — Get your Idea

You can get ideas for your choice of project from different places. Your teacher might:

1) tell you exactly what your task is.
2) give you a range of tasks to choose from.
3) leave the project choice completely up to you.

Don't choose anything Too Easy or Too Boring

Choose a project that will:

1) stretch you and let you demonstrate just how good you are. If the project's too easy, or contains little scope for design, then you'll lose valuable marks.
2) be interesting and challenging enough to keep you motivated. Coursework's a long old process, and you need to stay committed.
3) give you the opportunity to produce a wide range of research, and demonstrate your ICT skills.
4) allow for a variety of solutions, resulting in a project which can be completed before the deadline (and this includes allowing time for testing and evaluation).

The Design Brief — Give Loads of Detail

See page 1 for more on the design brief.

1) Your idea needs to have "real commercial potential".
2) You need to describe exactly what you're trying to do.
3) Explain all the factors you need to consider — things like price, weight, market trends, etc.

Say Why your Research is Relevant

1) DON'T just plonk bits of paper in your research folder without any explanation.
2) DON'T just copy and paste stuff from the Internet either.
3) DO write notes on every piece of research to say why it's relevant, how it changed your thinking or how it backed up your existing ideas.
4) DO refer back to the research section throughout the project — that helps to show you've used your research.

See page 2 for more on research.

THIS IS ALL YOU NEED TO DO:

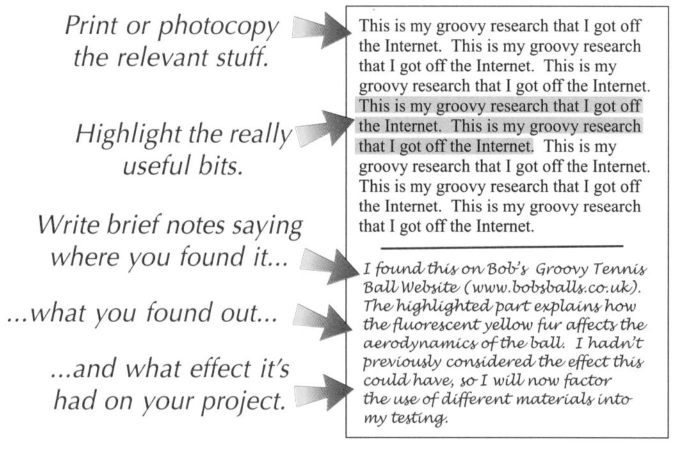

Print or photocopy the relevant stuff.
Highlight the really useful bits.
Write brief notes saying where you found it...
...what you found out...
...and what effect it's had on your project.
This is my groovy research that I got off the Internet. This is my groovy research that I got off the Internet. This is my groovy research that I got off the Internet. This is my groovy research that I got off the Internet. This is my groovy research that I got off the Internet. This is my groovy research that I got off the Internet. This is my groovy research that I got off the Internet.
I found this on Bob's Groovy Tennis Ball Website (www.bobsballs.co.uk). The highlighted part explains how the fluorescent yellow fur affects the aerodynamics of the ball. I hadn't previously considered the effect this could have, so I will now factor the use of different materials into my testing.

Remember — your research analysis will contain all the conclusions from research. But these notes will help you write that research analysis, and will also help the examiner understand why you made your decisions.

Tips on Development

If you're smart you'll keep planning and evaluating throughout your project. If you're a buffoon you'll do a bit at the start, then forget about it and get a bad mark for your project.

You Need a Wide Range of Ideas — Be Creative

1) There's more than one way to skin a cat.
2) Consider plenty of different ways to solve the problem.
3) Don't just come up with one good idea and stick with it. You'll only be sure it's the best idea if you've thought about other ways of doing it.
4) The examiners do really get annoyed about this one — so get those creative juices flowing.

Developing your Ideas — Try Out a Few Alternatives

1) The same goes for developing ideas as for creating them.
2) There's still more than one way to skin a cat.
3) Once you've got the idea, there are still plenty of ways to turn that into an ace product.

Do Loads of Planning — and Not Just at the Start

Planning is for life, not just for... um... the start of your project.
These are the things you should do:

OVERALL PROJECT PLAN AT THE START:

1) to help you focus on the task
2) to make sure you know what stage you should have reached at any time — this way, if you fall behind schedule, you'll know about it as soon as possible, and can do something about it
3) to allow enough time for all the different stages of the design process — including testing, evaluation, and writing up your project

Remember to include testing and evaluating in your time plan — it's all too easy to forget them...

PLAN YOUR RESEARCH:

Work out what research you need to do, and how long you're going to allow yourself for each bit (e.g. questionnaires, disassembling a competing product, and so on).

DON'T GET BOGGED DOWN:

When you're generating proposals or developing your product, don't spend too long working on one little aspect of the product. There's a lot to do — so try to keep your project moving forward.

I have a cunning plan...

OK, repeat after me: "I will allow time for testing in my time plan. I will allow time for testing in my time plan. I will allow time for testing in my time plan. I will allow time for testing in my time plan..."

Tips on Evaluation

Evaluation means examining and judging your work (and you have to do this as part of your project — it's not just something for the examiner to do). If your product doesn't work, but you explain why, you can still get good marks.

Test and Evaluate your Product Throughout the Project

I quote:

> *"To be achieving the highest marks in this section, candidates must show that they have used a clear and objective testing strategy."*

That's from one of the Chief Examiners' Reports.
(In other words, it's important.)

Don't Wait until you're Finished to Evaluate your Work

1) Like any designer, it's a good idea to be thinking about evaluation from the moment you start working on your design brief.
2) Make notes on your designs and developments as you go along, explaining what was good and bad about each one.
3) When you're writing up your final evaluation, you can also think about whether you'd do anything differently if you were starting again. It's okay if you made some bad decisions during your project — everyone does. But you can get marks if you explain why they were bad decisions, and what you wish you'd done instead.

Check your Brief and Specification

You need to evaluate your product fully. Use these guidelines:

1) Compare your final product to your brief and specification. Does your product satisfy all the conditions it's supposed to? If not, why not?
2) Try to get a likely user (or an expert in this kind of product, maybe) to trial your product and give their honest opinions. This will give you a realistic view of whether it's fit for its purpose — e.g. does it do what it's meant to? And if it does, how well? They may also be able to give you ideas for improvements.
3) It's also dead important to think about things you could have done better, such as...

① Time implications — did you spend too much time in one area, or rush to finish?

② Practical work — were you completely satisfied with the quality of your final product?

③ Would you approach aspects of your design and development work in a different way?

Never forget to check your briefs...

Everyone makes mistakes (well, everyone except me, obviously). More specifically, everyone makes mistakes in their projects. So don't worry too much when it happens to you.
Just explain what went wrong and how you'd avoid it in the future. You can get marks for that.

Tips on Presentation

It's no use doing a stonking project if your presentation's naff. You've put a lot of time and effort into your project (probably) so it would be a shame for you to mess it up at the last stage.

It really is worth putting in those few extra hours.

The Finished Product — Good Photographs are Ace

Your evaluation should be clearly presented and easy to read.

1) Include an introduction to give a bit of background information — e.g. how you came to think of the project.
2) Always take photos of any non-permanent work or intermediate stages in making the product. You can use either a normal or a digital camera and then either glue in the print or place the digital image into a word-processed document — whatever suits.

Photos are the only way of getting a lasting record of your work — and the examiners *REALLY WANT* you to do it.

3) Use a mixture of media to present your project. It's always good to show off how nifty you are with CAD or that desktop publishing program, but don't forget about old-fashioned words to explain what you did, and sketches and prototypes to show how you did it.
4) Split up your evaluation into different sections to make it easy to read.

   The sections could include:
   a) how well your product satisfies the brief and specification
   b) results from user trials
   c) problems you encountered
   d) improvements for the future

   Give each section a clear heading.

5) Think about how it fits together — your project needs to work *as a whole*. It should flow seamlessly from one bit to the next — don't just shove loads of separate bits in with no clue as to how they fit together.

Vocabulary — use the Right Technical Terms

BIG, FANCY WORDS:

1) Do yourself a favour — learn all the technical terms.
2) And how to spell them.
3) And don't worry if you sound poncy.
4) Using the right technical terms impresses the examiners. They say so in their reports.

GRAMMAR, SPELLING, PUNCTUATION:

1) Treat your project like an English essay.
2) Get your spellings right. Double-check any words you often get wrong.
3) Remember to use full stops and capital letters and write in proper sentences.
4) Short sentences make your work clearer. Long sentences, with loads of commas, can often get very confusing, because it's easy, once you get to the end of the sentence, to forget what you were reading right at the start.
5) Structure your work in paragraphs — a new paragraph for a new topic.

Santa cheats at presentation — he uses elves...

Of course your project has to look nice. I mean, what would you rather read... a beautifully presented folder of work, or something scribbled down on the back of a mucky paper towel...

Summary Checklist

This stuff can really make your project sparkle.
That's why I've given it a whole extra page — so you can't forget any of it.

Before you hand in your project, make sure you've covered all of these bits, and you'll be well on your way to Product Design heaven.

Sparkly Project Checklist

- ☐ 1) My design brief has loads of detail.
- ☐ 2) I've done plenty of research, and said why it's relevant.
- ☐ 3) I've made a detailed design specification.
- ☐ 4) I've come up with a wide range of project proposals.
- ☐ 5) I've included different ways of developing my product, and explained why I made my decisions.
- ☐ 6) I've tested my product on consumers.
- 7) I've done loads of planning, including:
  - ☐ a) a production plan (time plan),
  - ☐ b) planning for mass production.
- ☐ 8) I've evaluated my product throughout the project.
- ☐ 9) I've taken photos of intermediate stages and anything that won't last.
- ☐ 10) I've used a mixture of media to present my project.
- ☐ 11) I've checked my spelling and grammar.
- ☐ 12) I've used the right technical terms.

Index

A

A4 paper 36
accentuating shapes 14
accurate drawings 13
adhesives 56
advertising 11
aesthetics 4, 23, 24, 28
Allen keys 55
animal glue 56
annealing 40, 52
anthropometrics 26
apron 32
assembly 65
assembly drawings 18
audits and assessments 27
auger bits 49
automated 65

B

band saw 50
batch production 20, 63
bench grinder 50
bevel-edged 49
biodegradable 25-26
biological washing powders 27
black japan 55
blind rivets 56
blockboard 38
blocks 57
blow moulding 51, 53
blow torch 58
boards 36, 38
body measurement data 26
bolts 55
braces 49
brackets 57
bradawls 49
brainstorming 4
brand loyalty 28
brass 39
brass spelter 58
brazing 58
British Electrotechnical Approvals Board (BEAB) 29
British Standards Institute 29, 33
British Standards Kitemark 31, 33
British Toy and Hobby Manufacturers' Association 29
brittle 40
buildings 64
butt hinge 59
butt joint 57

C

cabinet rasps 49
CAD 13, 16, 19
CAM 20, 66
cams 47
car-body filler 60
carbohydrates 45
carbon fibre 42
carrying tools safely 32
cartridge paper 36
casting 32, 54
catches 59
CE mark 29
cell production 65
ceramics 43
chemical manufacture 63
chipboard 38
chisels 49
choking hazard 33
chuck keys 32
circular saw 50
clamping 32
clay 43
clearance holes 55
colour wheel 16
coloured pencils 15
communication 11, 64, 65
competition 25
complementary colours 16
composites 42, 61
compression moulding 51
concurrent engineering 65
consumer demand 23
consumer protection 29
Consumer Safety Act 29
consumers 11, 23, 29, 33
contact adhesive 56
continuous improvement 9
continuous production 63
continuous strips 54
control 66
Control Of Substances Hazardous to Health (COSSH) 33
coping saws 49
corrugated card 36
cost 7, 25, 28
cotton 44
cow gum 36
cranks 47
crating 12
critical temperature 40
cross-sections 4
cubes 13
customers 11, 19
customer research 1
customer satisfaction 29
cutting 49

D

David's Isopon 60
deburring metal 32
deciduous 37
deforming 52-53
degreasing metal 32
depth 14
design brief 1, 68
design methods 9
design process 1
design specification 3, 8, 67
designers 11
detachable components 33
details (of designs) 11-12, 18
developing ideas/designs 5, 25, 69
deviation 67
die casting 54
digital cameras 4, 21
disassembly 2, 25
disposal of waste 26-27, 32
don't be a moron 32
dot shading 14
dot-matrix printers 14
doughnuts 58
dovetail jig 51
dovetail joints 51, 57
dowel joint 57
down time 63
drawing programmes 19
drilling jig 51
drilling machines 20, 32
drills 49
drums (washing machines) 27
duplex board 36
dust extraction equipment 32

E

efficiency 51, 64
electric-arc welder 58
electrical components 46
emergency 32
emissions 27
empirical design 9
employers' responsibility 33
energy efficiency 27
engineers' lathes 50
enhancement 14-16
environment 25-27, 36
environmental audits 27
Environmental Health Department 29
environmental responsibility 26, 27
enzyme technology 27
epoxy resin 56
ergonomics 25-26
EU law 27
evaluation 5, 6, 29, 69-71
exploded drawings 18
extrusion 54
eye strain 26

F

fabrics 44
face masks 32
factory siting 27
fashion 11, 28
fat 45
felt-tips 36
ferrous 39
fibre 45
fibres 44
Fibonacci series 24
files 49
fillers 60
final product specification 3
finishing 7, 21, 60
fire safety regulations 29
firing 43
fittings/fixtures 59
flame cutters 20
flammable liquids 32
flat bits 49
flexible machinery and labour 63, 65
flexible manufacturing systems 65
flow charts 8
fluidised powder 40
flush hinges 59
flux 58
FMS (flexible manufacturing system) 65
foamboard 36
food 45
forge 52
form 25
formative evaluation 6
freehand sketching 4, 12
function 23, 24, 25, 34
functional requirements 34

G

Gantt chart 8
gaps in the market 1, 11
gas brazing torch 58
gauntlets 32
gears 47

Index

geometric shapes 12, 24
glass-reinforced plastic (GRP) 42
gloves 32
goats 16
goggles 32
green (environmentally friendly) 27
grids 13, 17
grid paper 13, 36
guidelines for drawing 12

H

hacksaws 49
halving joint 57
Hammerite 40
hand drills 49
hand tools 49
hardened threads 55
hardening 40
hardwood 37
harm 26
Hazard Analysis Critical Control Points (HACCP) 67
hazardous materials 32
health and safety 26, 32-33
Health and Safety at Work Act 33
heat treatments 40
hexagonal head 55
high speed steel (HSS) 49
highlights 14-15
highly skilled workforce 63
hinges 59
Holmes, Eamonn 54
horizon line 17
housing joint 57
HSS twist bits 50
hue 16
hydroelectricity 27

I

ideas 11, 21, 30
in-line assembly 65
industrial washing machines 27
injection moulding 54
inspiration 24
International Standards Organisation (ISO) 29
intuitive design 9
iron 39
isometric drawing/grid paper 12-13

J

jigs 51
jobbing production 63
joints 57
just-in-time 65

K

kids 26
Kitemark 31, 33
klett 36
knitted fabrics 44
knock-down fittings 57

L

labelling 29, 31
labour intensive 63
lacquers 40, 60
laminating 52, 60
laminboard 38
landfill 27
lap joint 57
lathes 20, 32, 50
laws 29, 33
leg fastenings 59
legislation 29
levers 47
life cycle assessments 27
light 14
linear motion 47
lines
- centre 18
- dimension 18
- outlines 18
- projection/construction 18

linkages 47
Local Authority Consumer Protection Department 29
Local Authority Trading Standards Officers 29
locks 59
logo 30
long hair tied back 32
long-term health impacts 26
looks 24
lower deviation 67
lycra 44

M

machine drills 49
machine screw 55
machine tools 50
made-to-measure furniture 63
maintenance 30
man-made fibres 44
manufacturer's specification 7
manufacturing 63-65
marker pens 15, 36
market 11
market pull 23
market research 6
market trends 2, 28
marking out 51
mass production 30, 63, 65
material 34
mathematics 24
MDF 38
measuring 2
metal ores 27
metal shavings 32
metal spikes 33
metals 15, 39-40, 54
micrometer 67
milling machine 50
minerals 45
misuse of products 26
mitred joint 57
mock-ups 11
modelling/models 3, 5, 11
modelling packages 19
Modroc 60
mood 16
mood board 4
moral issues 26-27
moron 32
mortise & tenon 57
mortise chisels 49
moulds 25, 51
mounting card 36

N

nail punch 56
nails 56
naked flames 32
National Consumer Council 29
National Federation of Consumer Groups 29
natural fibres 44
nature 24
new product 11
nitinol 42
non-ferrous 39
non-permanent joints 57
non-stop production 63
non-toxic 33
North European neighbours 27
nutritional information 31
nuts 55
nylon 44

O

office chair toilet 11
Office of Fair Trading 29
oil 27
oil manufacture 63
one-off product 63
one-point perspective 17
orthographic projection 4, 18
oscillating motion 47
other people's stuff 25
outlines 18
overlap of stages of production 65
oxidising 58
oxyacetylene torch 58

P

packaging 27, 61
pain and injury 26
paints/painting 37, 40, 60
pan handle 41
panel pin 56
paper 36
parents 26
patents 30
patterns 51
pedestal drill 50
peer pressure 11
pencils 14
perspective drawing/paper 4, 13, 17, 36
photographs 21, 71
pillar drill 50
pilot holes 55
pineapples 1
pivot hinge 59
plan views 18
planer 50
planes 49
planning 7-8, 69
Plaster of Paris 43, 61
plastic coating 40
plastics 15, 27, 41
plastizote 41
plywood 38, 52
polishing 40
pollution 27
polyfilla 61
polypropylene 27
polystyrene 41
polythene 41
pop rivets 56
porcelain 43
poster paints 15
pottery 43
power drill 49
presentation 71

Index

presentations 21
preservation (foods) 61
press moulding 53
primary colours 16
primer 41
processes 25
product standards 29
product analysis 25
projecting lines 17
promotion 61
protection during transit 61
protective clothing 32
protein 45
prototypes 5, 9, 11
pulleys 47
PVA 56

Q

quality assurance (QA) 29, 67
quality control (QC) 7-8, 29, 65, 67
questionnaires 2, 6, 8

R

rainforests 27
ratio 18
reciprocating motion 47
recording your work 21
recycling 26-27, 36, 61
reforming 54
rendering 14
renewable energy sources 27
repetitive shapes 51
repetitive tasks 63
research 2-3, 68-69
research analysis 2-3
resin 60
reusing 61
risk assessments 33, 64
risks 32
rivets 56
rotary motion 47
ruling guidelines 12

S

safe products 26, 33
safety 26, 31-33, 64
- instructions 31
- guards 32
- standards 33
- with tools and machinery 32
Sale Of Goods Act 29
saw bench 50
saws 49
scale drawings 18
scale of production 34, 63
school workshop 63
screwdrivers 55
screws 55
secondary colours 16
sectional drawings 18
self-tapping screws 55
semi-skilled workers 65
sensory analysis 2
sequence diagrams 7
shading 14-15
shanks 55-56
shape memory alloy 42
sheet metal 15, 52
shelving fitments 59
silicon 42
sketching 12-13, 71
slogans 61
small children 33
small components 33
smart materials 42
social responsibility 26
softwood 37
soldering 58
solid white board 36
space shuttles 43
spats 32
splinters 37
split die 55
spreadsheets 7
square grid paper 13, 36
standards 29, 33, 67
steel 39-40
stockpiles 65
structure 24
summative evaluation 8
surface finish 40
surfaces (drawing) 15
surveys 8
sustainable resources 36
systematic design 9
systems 46, 64-66

T

tamper-evident seals 61
taps 55
target customers 11
teams/teamwork 63, 65
technological push 23
tee hinges 59
teeth 49
telephones 23
tempering 40
templates 51
tenon saws 49
testing 5, 9, 70
textiles 44
texture 14-15, 45
thermoplastics 41, 53-54
thermosetting plastic powder 53
thermosetting plastics 41, 53
thicknesser 50
threading 55
threatened resources 27
TIG welder 58
tolerances 7, 67
tones 14
toxic paint or varnish 26, 33
toys 33
tracing paper 36
Trade Descriptions Acts 29
trademarks 30
tufnol 42
turnips 1
twist bits 49
two-point perspective 17

U

unskilled labour 63, 65
user-friendly products 26

V

vacuum forming 51, 53
value for money 25, 29
vanishing points 17
vapours 32
varnish 26, 33, 37, 60
vehicle for paint pigment 60
veneers 38
ventilation 32
vitamins 45

W

washing machines 27
waste 26-27, 32, 61, 64
watercolour paints 15
welding 58
wind power 27
wireframe 13
woad 60
wood 15, 36-37, 55-56
- grain 15
- lathes 50
- screws 55
- stain 37
wool 44
work order 8
working drawings 7, 18
woven fabrics 44

Y

yarns 44